The
Accidental
Manager

The Accidental Manager

Get the Skills You Need to Excel in Your New Career

Gary S. Topchik

AMACOM

American Management Association

New York • Atlanta • Brussels • Chicago • Mexico City
San Francisco • Shanghai • Tokyo • Toronto • Washington, D. C.

This publication is designed to provide accurate and authoritative information in regard to the subject matter covered. It is sold with the understanding that the publisher is not engaged in rendering legal, accounting, or other professional service. If legal advice or other expert assistance is required, the services of a competent professional person should be sought.

Library of Congress Cataloging-in-Publication Data

Topchik, Gary S.
    The accidental manager : get the skills you need to excel in your new career / Gary S. Topchik.— 1st ed.
        p. cm.
Includes index.
    ISBN 0-8144-7180-3
    1. Management. I. Title.

HD31.T6368 2003
658.4'09—dc21
                                            2003011085

Printing number

10 9 8 7 6 5 4 3 2 1

Dedicated to the memory of

MARTY TOPCHIK

Contents

Acknowledgments   ix

Introduction   1

Chapter 1.   You Are an Accidental Manager
             (That's Okay)   7

Chapter 2.   The All-Time Worst Manager List   17

Chapter 3.   The Key to Success: "Doing Nothing"   35

Chapter 4.   The Platinum Skill of Developing
             Your Team Members   49

Chapter 5.   The Platinum Skill of Active Listening   71

Chapter 6.   The Platinum Skill of Giving and
             Receiving Feedback   99

Chapter 7.   The Platinum Skill of Creating a
             Motivational Climate   129

Chapter 8.   How Organizations Can Turn Accidental
             Managers Into Successful Ones   159

Appendix A. Managerial Assessment   167

Index   173

Acknowledgments

I am most grateful to my business partners at SilverStar Enterprises and many other colleagues who saw a need for this book and motivated me to write it. I also want to thank all of the individuals I have met over the years in my consulting, executive coaching, and seminar practice. They shared with me their stories about being accidental managers. Their examples have been the foundation for this book.

I am also grateful to Len Bloom, who got me to a place in my life and career where I was motivated to put my words, beliefs, and experiences in writing. In addition, I would like to thank all the organizations that allowed me to be their keynote speaker and talk about the reality of the accidental manager.

My editor, Adrienne Hickey, deserves a tremendous amount of recognition for her support, patience, and encouragement. I would also like to thank Roberta Garcia for keeping me going toward the end of the writing. Finally, to the kids, SJ and Gersh, for just being themselves. They were very loving throughout the process.

The Accidental Manager

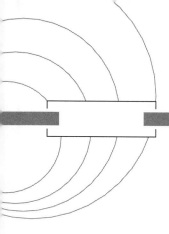

Introduction

Every day many individuals just like you are promoted into the ranks of management not ready to be—or even wanting to be—managers. You halfheartedly agree to the promotion if you want to stay employed within your organizations and/or make more money. You are almost always exceptional at what you do technically; that is why you got the promotion. Often, though, you really aren't interested in managing people. More than that, you may have no clue about how to manage people. You are an accidental manager. If given a choice, you would rather stick to the job you've been doing. After all, years ago, when asked what you wanted to be when you grow up, did you or any of the other accidental managers out there ever dream of saying, "I want to be a manager"?

The Accidental Manager has a simple message for you: It is okay not to want to be a manager of people. Management isn't necessarily the desired profession or career for everyone. However, if it is your decision to make the most of your situation, this book will help you survive, and survive extremely well, while in the managerial role. This book gives you the tools you need to succeed as a manager, once you realize that it is easier, more rewarding, and less time-consuming to manage well than to manage poorly.

The idea for this book evolved over the past fifteen years while I was working on many different organizational consulting projects and facilitating management seminars. During this time, I met many managers who were accidental ones.

The Accidental Manager provides practical examples of how to manage effectively, once you have overcome your resistance to the job. Only when you decide to manage well can you lose the title "accidental manager" and succeed in becoming a successful manager. The examples and case studies in this book are based on real situations I have encountered. Being an accidental manager is a universal phenomenon. It is not specific to any industry or country. I have found and worked with accidental managers in every type of work environment throughout the world.

The Accidental Manager has eight chapters and an appendix section. Chapter 1 presents a case study of an engineer who has been very successful in his job. Because of his success, he moved into a managerial role with a substantial salary increase. The engineer soon realized that this new role required many skills that he was neither trained for nor interested in acquiring. This book discusses the reasons why this engineer and thousands of others in similar situations become accidental managers, and the dilemmas they face.

Chapter 2 describes ten unsuccessful types of managers, with advice on how to avoid becoming one of them. These managers negatively impact the success of their team members, their departments, and the organization. I call them the All-Time Worst Manager types.

Chapter 3 focuses on how to succeed in your new managerial role, even if you accidentally fell into it. The chapter explains the differences among managing, leading, and doing. Successful and smart managers realize early on that what makes managing difficult is "the doing." The key to success is to spend one's day managing and leading. I call it the "do nothing" approach. Once you learn the "do nothing" approach and become successful at it, you can then go back and do the things you want or need to, including your own projects. The approach allows you to stay current in the latest technology in your field (which can be difficult for managers who don't learn to delegate), or take on new projects from management. You may even become great at managing because you will no longer feel like an accidental manager. Chapter 3 also gives many tips on how to get started on the road to managing successfully and how to enjoy this new role.

The theme of Chapter 4 is developing your staff members by having them learn to work on their own and with other team members. If you can achieve this target, you will have the time to work on your own projects and the assignments you really like doing. If you are able to diagnose exactly what is needed to get each of your team members to succeed, then you and the organization will succeed as well. Developing others is essential to being able to become a successful manager. It is also the first of the Platinum skills, or the crucial skills for accidental managers to learn in order to become successful managers.

Chapters 5, 6, and 7 look at three other Platinum skills for successful management and leadership. In Chapter 5, the focus is on active listening. This skill increases your effectiveness in communicating with your team members and builds trust between you and your team. Chapter 6 covers the Platinum skill of giving both positive and constructive feedback, and learning how to receive feedback constructively from others. Feedback allows you to keep your team members on track so they can succeed. Chapter 7 focuses on the skill of motivating, which is providing the best possible environment for each team member to develop to his fullest. Being able to achieve excellence in these Platinum skills will allow you to focus on managing and leading your team members.

Chapter 8 discusses the negative impact that unsuccessful managers have on the organization and gives suggestions for what organizations can do to increase the success of their managers. The chapter also revisits the case study of the engineer from Chapter 1 to see what has happened to the case's protagonist, Andy Mercado.

I wrote *The Accidental Manager* for three major reasons. The first is to help you, or any other accidental managers, understand that there is absolutely nothing wrong in feeling or thinking like an accidental manager. The second is to have you gain confidence in your ability to manage and, therefore, change your perspective on what managing really means. Third, while consulting with a wide variety of clients for many years, I have uncovered a major, largely unexamined barrier to successful organizational performance: the unwillingness of many managers, accidental or not, to manage effectively.

Organizations need to recognize and develop strategies for overcoming this most costly barrier.

As mentioned previously, the main theme of *The Accidental Manager* is to show the reader how to succeed in a managerial role, even if you are there without expecting to be, or wanting to be, a manager in the first place. Why not turn this "accidental" opportunity into a big bonus for you and your company?

This book will inform you about:

✔ The many barriers that contribute to an individual's not wanting to be in a managerial role

✔ The specific skills and behaviors necessary to manage others well

✔ How to manage well without giving up your passion for the actual work

✔ How not to punish your excellent performers

✔ The types of managerial behaviors to avoid and how to prevent being viewed as a bad manager

✔ How to develop your people instead of rescuing them

✔ How to determine the productivity stage for each of your team members

✔ The communication and active-listening strategies for building trust and loyalty with and among your team members

✔ How to train and delegate staff so they can work independently and interdependently

✔ How not to reward your poorer performers

✔ The differences between leading, managing, and doing—and how to do more of the leading and managing and less of the doing

✔ The different strategies for providing an environment where your staff can be motivated

✔ How to keep your team members on track and greatly reduce performance and behavioral problems

✔ How to enjoy the unexpected opportunity of being part of the management team

✔ How to give positive feedback and reward your team members

Here's a suggestion: When reading the book, don't think that every strategy, tip, or technique will work equally well for you. Be selective. Use the ideas that will work best for you!

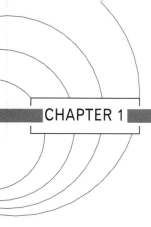

CHAPTER 1

You Are an Accidental Manager (That's Okay)

Meet Andy Mercado

I would like to introduce you to Andy Mercado. Andy is a great guy, well liked by everyone, bright, energetic, hardworking, and respected by upper management. Andy graduated from the University of Michigan seven years ago with a degree in engineering. He has been steadily employed, at increasing salaries, at two different companies in the Seattle area.

Andy loves his job and especially enjoys his current project. He is working on a software development team that is designing new safety procedures for air traffic controllers. This software will allow the controllers to respond more quickly to potential emergencies. Andy likes the camaraderie of his team members. The team is given a great deal of autonomy on the project and the project manager most always agrees with the team's recommendations.

Andy was married two years ago, and he and his wife Lisa just adopted twins. Lisa is a fashion magazine editor currently on leave from her job. Both Andy and Lisa are avid speed skaters. That's how they met. Andy was number one on his college team and almost made the Olympic speed-skating team.

Andy rarely misses a day at the office. He feels that he is building his skills and developing his future potential while at work.

Six Months Later

I would like to reintroduce you to Andy Mercado. He is a changed man and tough to figure out. On some days he seems to get along with everyone and is very upbeat, much like the Andy of six months ago. Other days, however—and these times are increasing—he is moody and withdrawn and has occasional bursts of anger. His team members are beginning to avoid him because they never know what to expect from him. Only six months ago he was a top producer; now his work is marginal.

He has been working at the same manufacturing company for three years and has always received excellent performance appraisals. Last week he received a rating of "needs improvement" on his quarterly performance review. The areas where he was rated poorly include leadership abilities, organizational commitment, cooperativeness with staff, and willingness to develop staff.

Lisa has noticed some big changes in Andy at home as well in recent months. He seems lethargic about going to work in the mornings and often comes home for a couple of hours during the day to "escape," as he says. Even though he is home more, he spends less time with the twins. He also passes up opportunities to go speed skating, something he has never done before. Lisa is quite concerned about these changes in Andy's behavior and has tried to get him to talk about what is going on. She has imagined the worse. When she asks him what's up, all he ever says is that it is "the change" at work that is making him miserable.

The Change

Two months earlier (in April) Janice Styles, the vice president of the division for which Andy works, asked Andy to come to see her. She said she had great news. When Andy arrived for the meeting, Janice greeted him enthusiastically. He immediately knew something was up because Janice is a serious person and rarely shows strong positive emotions. Janice told him that he was doing a fantastic job and was the most knowledgeable member on the team, that all his colleagues admired and liked him a lot. She also told him that Ben Cline, his immediate boss, had been offered a position with another company and was leaving at the end of next week. Then she shared the great news. "You are getting promoted to Ben's job. You will be the new manager and will receive a 20 percent pay increase. Congratulations!"

Andy smiled and thanked Janice for the confidence that she had in him and said he welcomed the challenge. But when he walked out of her office, he felt quite distressed. He began to question what he had just agreed to. What did he know about managing? Did he want to be a manager? Didn't managers put company goals first and their professional passion second? Didn't the "guys" on the team goof on managers? In their view, people became managers to avoid the hard stuff. Was he old enough to be a manager? Most of the people he would be supervising were older than him. Did he know enough technically to manage all the diverse jobs of those who would now report to him?

What happened to Andy when he left Janice's office was that he experienced many of the classic trepidations of accidental managers. Accidental managers are often in a state of dissonance. They feel they have to accept these managerial roles because they are next in line for the job and senior management expects it of them. However, they really don't want to take on administrative or "people" responsibilities. Adding to their dissonant state of mind is the knowledge that they will get a nice pay raise and some special privileges.

Andy's reaction was quite normal and represents the reactions of hundreds of thousands of others in similar situations. According to surveys conducted by the management department at UCLA, over 80 percent of individuals who get promoted would rather have not accepted the promotion, for many of the same reasons expressed by Andy. They wish they could grow and develop in their current job roles and get rewarded appropriately, without taking on any managerial responsibilities.

Where's Andy Today?

Andy took the manager's job last April. He felt the company was counting on him, and with the adoption of the twins, he could use the extra money. The promotion didn't work out, however. He resented the new responsibilities and didn't know how to manage and lead the team. He was inconsistent in his management approach. Sometimes he would micromanage his team, telling them exactly what to do. When that backfired, he would avoid contact with them. He missed his old job and the fun he had. He missed hanging out with the "guys" from his team. He missed being involved in the work on a day-to-day basis. The company gave him the management job but not the training, support, or guidance he required.

Andy resigned last month. He couldn't take the pressures of managing. He was too embarrassed to ask for his old job back. Because of his technical background, proven skills, and determination, he obtained a nonmanagerial job at another organization. Andy is quite happy again!

Here's the message I have for those of you who are accidental managers: You have every right to feel the way you do! It is admirable to recognize and admit that you are not comfortable or happy as a manager. Respect your feelings and thoughts. However, the worst thing to do is to remain ambivalent about taking on a managerial role without wanting it. It can be deadly.

You basically have three options when you find yourself in the position of being, or about to become, an accidental manager:

Option 1. Refuse the promotion or the move into a managerial role and stay where you are, if that is what you want to do. If "they" put a lot of pressure on you to accept, you may have to leave that department or your organization. Option 1 is definitely a viable choice. Far too few accidental managers select this choice.

Option 2. Take on the new title in name only and don't be too concerned about managing. You can try not to let the managerial duties interfere with the work you are really interested in doing. And you can spend wasted time lamenting your fate. Option 2 is not recommended. It does your staff and company harm and, ultimately, you won't feel good about yourself. You'll become miserable, and in your mind, you will always be an accidental manager.

Option 3. Learn to succeed and become an excellent manager, even though you started out as an accidental one. You can do this by learning and practicing the key strategies and skills presented in this book. You can come to enjoy and be stimulated by this unexpected opportunity. Option 3 will be our focus.

Accidental Manager Myths

Let's now explore, in more specific terms, how Option 3 works. We will start with the most prevalent beliefs or myths as to why individuals become accidental managers in the first place. If you believe these myths to be true, then you will always feel and act like an accidental manager. The stories that follow are real.

Myth 1: "I am more comfortable with my current work than I will ever be with managing."
—Sheila W., manager at a pharmaceutical company, Piscataway, NJ

Of course you are, Sheila! Golfers are more comfortable with golf than with tennis. Managing, once you learn how to do it, is not that difficult and doesn't have to be that time-consuming. You have to learn new skills and behaviors. Once you start managing, your comfort level will increase greatly.

Tarj Sullivan Case Study

Take the true story of Tarj Sullivan. Ten years ago he was promoted to assistant bank manager from a teller position at his local branch office. He panicked. He had incredible anxiety attacks. He convinced himself that he could never feel comfortable doing anything besides being a teller. Tarj is now the manager of his bank. When I spoke with him a few months ago he said, "I couldn't believe how easy it was to manage, once I learned how." Tarj learned, most important, that he had to get to know his people, build a trusting relationship with them, listen to their concerns, get their input, and develop their skills and talents. When Tarj made these efforts with his staff, they knew that he was really concerned about them.

Myth 2: "Managing my friends will be impossible to do."
—Dennis S., manager for a credit card company, Monterrey, CA

Ridiculous. There are many managers who have friends—even their best friends—working for them. Not being able to successfully manage one's friends is surely one of the most popular myths. In fact, most of the excellent managers I've interviewed say that their employee friends perform extremely well for them. It happens every day that someone is promoted out of their peer group where they have close friends or must take on a managerial job where existing friends work. Just keep the following in mind when managing friends: There can be no special deals, no access to information that others aren't getting, no promises to provide them with better laptops, no biased performance appraisals, etc. Treat friends like everyone else during working hours by discussing and setting very clear boundaries.

Brandon Lester Case Study

Brandon proved that it is possible to manage employees who also happen to be friends. A few years ago Brandon was promoted to marketing manager. One of his newly inherited employees, Matt, was his best friend. Everyone in the company knew of their friendship. Brandon and Matt would always hang out together, both in the office and outside of work. When Brandon first took on his new role, he let the friendship get in the way of his managing. He would look the other way when Matt did not follow company procedures or standards. I remember Brandon telling me this story right after he became an accidental manager: One Tuesday morning after a three-day weekend, Matt showed up at the plant about two hours late. When Brandon asked Matt why he was late, Matt replied, "You know where we were last night. . ." Brandon laughed it off and walked away. He thought he was just being a good friend. A few hours later, though, he realized that to gain the respect he needed to be a successful manager he had to have the same standards for all of his staff. He had a long talk with Matt, discussing their friendship and how it was important to him. He also outlined how both he and Matt needed to work together as manager/employee. Ever since that talk, Brandon and Matt's working relationship has been fine and no other staff member has ever had reason to complain that Matt was getting preferential treatment. They are still the best of friends.

Myth 3: "Managing people who know more than I do will be an impossible situation. I will not be able to control them."
—*Alida S., manager for a large oil company, Eagle Rock, TX*

In most fields today, it is not realistic to believe that you can be the expert in everything. We have to rely on other people. In fact, if you trust your team and they are aware of that trust, you have it made. Ask them for their input and make the decisions together, or even better, let them make decisions on their own. Trying to control people is incredibly time-consuming, stressful for you and your employees, and quite unproductive. You should feel quite lucky if your staff members are experts in what they do.

Bob McCord Case Study

I once worked with a particularly strong accidental manager, Bob McCord. He hated when his people were more knowledgeable than he was. He wanted to be able to control all their moves. He purposely did not send them to training classes and would not share much of his knowledge with them. But he was overwhelmed all the time because he wound up doing all of their jobs. Bob would always say he hated managing. Of course he did. He wasn't managing. He was doing the work for the entire group.

Bob was a victim of the *fallacy of omnipotence.* He believed that he was the only one who could do certain things right or do them best. If you believe in this fallacy, you are going to be susceptible to burnout and stress-related illness. Let's face it. The truth is that there are others out there who could do a job as well as you, or maybe even better, with a little training. Managing people who know more than you do is something you should strive for. It will make the job of managing much easier and more enjoyable.

Myth 4: "If I take on the manager's job, not only will I have to do that, but I will still have most of my current work to do as well. I will never be able to do both well."
—*Carmine T., manager for a CPA firm, Miami, FL*

Of all the myths of managing, this is probably the one held by most accidental managers. The thought of having to manage a staff and still do all of your own work is definitely overwhelming. In fact, many accidental managers try to do both and fail miserably. And that makes them feel even more like accidental managers. Most companies require that their first-line supervisors and middle-level managers assume individual responsibilities and management responsibilities at the same time. Usually about 70 percent of their time is spent managing and 30 percent is devoted to individual duties. Throughout the book, there are ideas to help accidental managers figure out how to manage both of these major responsibilities. If managers can develop their staffs, actively listen, give and receive feedback, and motivate their employees, then they will have the time to manage and lead successfully. When managers are successful, they have the time to work on the projects assigned to them.

Brenda Garcia Case Study

Brenda was an accidental manager at a large public relations company in Salt Lake City. When she became a manager she was told that she would be expected to maintain most of her current accounts plus supervise the accounts of eight others. She was uneasy at this prospect, but the 30 percent salary increase eased her reluctance. For the first few months of her management career, Brenda could not do both jobs effectively. Sometimes she would focus only on her work to the detriment of her staff. Other times she focused only on their accounts to the detriment of hers.

Brenda soon realized that if she gave her staff the necessary skills to do their jobs well, and gave them the confidence and motivation to want to do what they were supposed to, their productivity improved greatly. When her staff members were able to do more and were happy doing it, Brenda could focus more of her time on her own projects. She had to do much less fire-fighting and rescuing, both of which are time-consuming. Brenda learned that it's possible to manage well and, at the same time, work on her own projects.

Myth 5: "I will no longer be able to keep up with the latest trends and current advances in my field if I am managing."
—*Bernie H., manager for a wire and cable company, Bethesda, MD*

When a person learns how to manage by "doing nothing," he can easily keep up with the latest in his field. Doing nothing means you get as much of the work of your group/unit/department, and your own work, done through your team(s). Then you are freed up to do many other things, such as keeping up with the latest research and advancements in your professional field and spending more time managing and leading. The more time you have to manage and lead, the more you will be able to keep up with the trends in your field. (The "do nothing" philosophy is described in Chapter 3.)

Bob Rosen Case Study

A former accidental manager, Bob Rosen, related this story to me: About five years ago, when Bob was first promoted into a managerial slot at his high-tech company in the San Francisco Bay area, he feared that he was going to fall behind technologically. He obsessed so much about this that he came to work two hours earlier each day to meet with different members of his team who would educate him on the latest trends. Not a bad idea, though it cost the company a lot of money in staff overtime.

Months into his tenure as a manager, Bob realized that he could still keep up with the latest trends. He learned how to "do nothing!" He developed his staff to do as much of the department's work as possible. He developed them by training them, delegating to them, and supporting their efforts. Even though Bob still had to do the projects that he was assigned, he had more time to review the current research findings in his field, and manage and lead.

Chapter Summary

Moving into a managerial role without really wanting to be in that position makes you an accidental manager. It is fine and even admirable to admit that you are an accidental manager. It is not good, however, to continue in the management role if you really don't want to manage.

If you decide to continue along the management path, even temporarily, you will need certain skills to be successful. Those skills, known as Platinum skills, include developing the capabilities of your staff, actively listening, giving and receiving feedback, and creating a workplace environment that motivates people. (Platinum skills are discussed in Chapters 4–7.) Additionally, in order for accidental managers to succeed they need to learn how to "do nothing." By learning the "do nothing" approach (Chapter 3) and acquiring Platinum skills, you can become comfortable in your new managerial role. You will be able to manage all people well, even friends and people who know more than you do technically. You'll also be able to balance your individual responsibilities with your management ones, and stay current with the latest trends and advances in your field.

CHAPTER 2

The All-Time Worst Manager List

When individuals take on a supervisory or managerial role and do not succeed in it, they can find themselves on the "All-Time Worst Manager List." This chapter identifies the seven worst manager types and offers advice on how to avoid turning into any one of them. At their worst, these managers demoralize their staff and negatively impact the productivity and/or profitability of their departments and organizations. Any manager, accidental or not, can wind up on this list. And there are many other bad manager types as well. It seems, however, that accidental managers gravitate toward these ten bad management habits:

1. The Non-Communicator
2. The Management Knocker
3. The Task Monger
4. The Best Friend
5. The Limelight Taker
6. The Self-Castigator
7. The Waffler
8. The Braggart
9. The Deceiver
10. The Exaggerator Congratulator

The Non-Communicator: The Carl Long Case

A few years ago Carl was a production assistant at a Los Angeles–based film and television studio. He liked his job and enjoyed working on the different sets. He was on a union list waiting appointment as a cameraman, his long-term ambition. However, he needed to earn more money while he was awaiting his appointment (which sometimes can take years), so he applied for a production supervisor job. To his surprise, he got the appointment. He knew little about managing and really had no interest in assuming this level of work. His studio offered no advice or training on supervising and just promoted him. Carl's reaction to his situation was to stop communicating with the people he was meant to supervise.

Symptoms of the Non-Communicator. A non-communicator is not sociable and isn't interested in exchanging ideas, thoughts, or opinions. These managers are secretive and impossible to read; they have a closed-door policy, avoid holding meetings, and even walk past people as if in a trance, showing only blank stares. Verbal responses are one or two words with a hurry-up, "get this over fast" attitude.

Impact on Staff. Staff members will feel a non-communicator doesn't care and isn't concerned about them or their jobs. After a while employees will discount the manager and try to get what they need from someone else. If they cannot do that, they will come to resent their non-communicator manager, their jobs, and the organization.

Impact on Department/Organization. Productivity declines, turnover increases, and there is loss of company pride.

Why Accidental Managers Become Non-Communicators. They are uncomfortable in their new roles because they are not sure how they are supposed to communicate with their staff. They are not sure if they should be strict or friendly. They have never gotten the management and communication skills training needed and may never have worked for an effective manager. They have not had a positive role model. Because they are not sure how to communicate, they don't.

Hints for the Non-Communicator. It is very important not to close down the channels of communication. Non-communicators can avoid doing this in a few ways. First, it is okay for the new manager to admit that he is new to supervision and that it will take him some time to become proficient. Second, the manager must come across as being genuinely interested in how employees are doing. The manager needs to speak to the staff, ask them how things are going, give them positive feedback when they do well, and offer suggestions to improve their quality of work. Third, the manager must set goals with each staff member, then follow up; that means constantly communicating with staff members on how they are achieving these goals. Their goals should align with the goals of the department and/or organization.

When managers are receiving information from their staff, they need to make sure they understand the information and they must let the staff know that the information has been understood. Managers can ask questions, clarify what they heard, and summarize. They need to pay close attention not only to the verbal content of their own messages and the messages of others, but to the nonverbal signals they send as well (e.g., their body language and tone of voice).

The Management Knocker: The Tina Nieves Case

Tina works for a plastic manufacturing company outside of Dallas. She knew that eventually she would be promoted to a management-level job. It happens to everyone who's been there long enough. It happened to her last Thursday. Tina has been with the organization for fifteen years. At her company, salary is based on productivity. Tina has been an outstanding employee in terms of her production and has always been handsomely rewarded for it. Now, as manager, she will no longer have her own work to do. She "just has to make sure that her team members meet their productivity levels" each week.

Tina could have refused the promotion, but the culture of the organization wouldn't permit that. It is her turn and she has to accept it. She will probably even make less money now because she used to get paid double to work weekends or holidays. Managers at her company get a base salary no matter how many hours they work. She has absolutely no aspirations of moving up the management ladder (in fact, that is her biggest fear). Tina feels as if she is stuck for the next couple of years. She can retire early and lose much of her pension or she can wait it out for a few years, when the company will rotate someone else into the managerial role and she can go back to her former position. Meanwhile, Tina handles her situation by negating the importance of the management role.

> *Symptoms of the Management Knocker.* A Management Knocker ridicules the management role by saying that anyone can be a manager and that managers' jobs are not important. These individuals put themselves down for being in that role and tease those in higher-level positions by pointing out that they aren't doing "real work." They don't hide their feelings or thoughts about not wanting to be in their new managerial role.

> *Impact on Staff.* As a result of this behavior, staff members don't respect the management role, do not aspire to be in it, and get a skewed picture of what managing really means.

> *Impact on Department/Organization.* In the vast majority of organizations, there is a direct correlation between effective management and bottom-line results. In this case, even though the organization seems to be doing fine, imagine how much better it could do with professional managers who were respected by their teams. Managers who practice "pass-through management" (i.e., blaming others, ridiculing the organization, belittling the managerial role) eventually impact the performance of their departments and companies. When managers practice pass-through management, it indirectly gives their staff permission to also criticize the department, company, senior managers, and customers. After all, if their managers are blaming and criticizing, they can do it as well. These pass-through behaviors eventually impact the morale and the quality of staff productivity. Managers, accidental or not, need to disavow the practice of pass-through management. They need to openly communicate their support for organizational procedures, policies, and practices, even if they may disagree with them.

> For example, a manager supports the organization's current computer system and feels that the new system the organization wants to purchase is not as good. Her team members know she favors the present system. The manager needs to tell her team that even though she prefers the current system, she will do

everything to guarantee the success of the new system, and that she will expect everyone on the team to do the same.

Why Accidental Managers Become Management Knockers. They knock management and/or organizational policies because, in essence, they are denying that they are now having to do what they never wanted or expected to be doing in the first place—managing.

Hints for the Management Knocker. Communicate to your team that although managing was not your original career choice, you are going to be the best possible manager. Always speak about your department/organization in constructive terms. Once you start putting down the organization, you give license to your people to do the same. Also, talk about the job of managing—the challenges and the rewards that one can get from managing. It could influence your own attitude about managing.

Many accidental managers come to appreciate the job of managing. This occurs when they see their staff or their department accomplishing goals, meeting customer demands, or making a difference in the larger community. The greatest thrill managers can have is realizing the impact that they have had on their staff. When managers see how their staff has grown and developed and become indispensable to the department or organization, they truly feel successful and enjoy the management job.

The Task Monger: The Jennifer James Case

Jennifer would do very well working with robots. Her focus is strictly on task and making sure her employees do exactly what they are supposed to. She never listens to her team, asks for their thoughts or opinions, or gives them the morale boost they need. She is all task focused. Her favorite phrase is, "I want it yesterday."

When Jennifer applied for an engineering job at a Miami navigation services company she did not expect that she would be managing others. But a few months into her tenure, the company received a most lucrative contract in Jennifer's field of expertise. She now supervises a team of eleven. She would rather be doing the research. Jennifer believes managers must be tough and firm, like drill sergeants, if they are to get what they need from their people. She doesn't have time for all this "relationship-building stuff" that her human resources manager keeps telling her to do. After all, she is managing a group of highly trained professionals who should be able to do what they are expected to do. If they did not want an expert at the helm of this project, let them find someone else. Besides, she did not want to be managing in the first place.

Symptoms of the Task Monger. Task Mongers rarely smile or change their facial expressions. They look stern and unhappy. They tend to micromanage, want it "their way or the highway," and expect everyone to agree with their unilateral decision making. Their voice is often monotone with little inflection, except when a deadline is approaching and they have not gotten what they need. Then they explode.

Impact on Staff. Staff members tend to perform because they have to and not because they want to, especially if they are fearful of losing their job or getting yelled at in front of others. The Task Monger's staff would perform better if they got some encouragement and inspiration, were listened to, and were empowered to make decisions.

Impact on Department/Organization. In organizations where there is strictly a task focus, stress is high and burnout is prevalent. The stressful environment eventually effects individuals' abilities to perform at their peak levels; it can also lead to high turnover, absenteeism, and increased health problems.

Why Accidental Managers Become Task Mongers. The most difficult part of managing is focusing on the people skills, sometimes called the supportive skills. New managers have little or no practice in the supportive skills of motivating, listening, coaching, and encouraging. Therefore, they rely on what they know—the task skills—how to do the work and get the job done. They do not understand that the supportive people skills are just as important as the task or directive behaviors. Both skill sets are needed to maintain a high level of morale and productivity over long periods of time. Being supportive means encouraging teamwork, involving team members in decision making, listening to team members' concerns, explaining reasons for actions or decisions, sharing information about the department or organization, sharing one's thoughts and feelings, and reassuring team members when they doubt their abilities or feel overburdened.

Hints for the Task Monger. Managers need to try to be supportive by encouraging their team members, getting them involved in decision making that impacts their work, and giving them a lot of recognition when they deserve it. Managers also need to ensure that they have understood what their employees are really saying to them, not what they want them to say. To achieve that understanding, they need to become good listeners. Being a good listener is more than simply hearing what staff members say; it means paying attention to the content of the message and the feelings behind the message. Managers will find that by demonstrating more of these supportive skills they will get the performance they need much easier than just by being a Task Monger.

The Best Friend: The Michael Jaffe Case

Like so many others, Michael was transferred from his group to another group where he was asked to take on managerial responsibilities. Like Andy Mercado, whose story was presented in Chapter 1, Michael was technically proficient and the best qualified of the existing staff. The organization for which Michael works also believes in promoting from within. Michael feels quite insecure about his management skills. He had never really considered management as a career. He considers himself a Web designer and would rather do that than manage others.

Michael's approach to managing is to become a best friend. He wants to fit in with the group, avoid causing any waves, and be well liked by all. He feels if the team likes him and treats him like "one of the guys," there will be few problems.

Symptoms of the Best Friend. The Best Friend manager looks the other way when work is late or procedures are not being followed. He makes excuses for team members and never confronts them. He socializes with his team both at work and outside the office. He is always cheerful and smiling, trying not to take anything too seriously. Relationship building is a big part of the Best Friend approach to managing. Somehow the work will get done. Michael feels if he is well liked, he will never run into any negative issues with his team.

Impact on Staff. Even though they would not admit it to their "best friend" managers, most staff members like to have direction, know what their limits and boundaries are, and have their managers develop, direct, guide, and educate them. When this does not occur, they begin to look for other individuals within the group or organization who can mentor and set goals for them. Lacking that, they will look to leave the organization.

Impact on Department/Organization. The Best Friend scenario is often referred to as the social work group. This is a group of individuals who like each other and get along extremely well, but they do not focus on accomplishing the goals set by the organization. Instead, they have their own priorities that do not align with the priorities of the organization. Eventually, Michael's Best Friend behavior will backfire on him. The work will not get done, or it won't get done as well or as quickly and efficiently as it should. Another impact is that team members will begin to identify solely with Michael and their other teammates. Although you want staff to feel this bond, their primary focus should always be on the goals of the department and organization.

Why Accidental Managers Become Best Friends. By becoming a best friend, managers hope to avoid confrontation and as many hassles, disagreements, and conflicts as possible. They think that just by being the best friend, everyone will like them no matter how inadequate they are in their new managerial role.

Hints for the Best Friend. It is fine to be friends or friendly with the people you manage. But the work, and the business, must always come first. Explain to your staff what you expect from them, what they can expect from you, what their goals are, and how you plan on working together with them. Emphasize that the quality, quickness, and quantity (the 3Qs) of their work should be everyone's primary focus in the workplace. The 3Qs are a way of identifying three of the major responsibilities of the manager. A manager must always be concerned that the service or product that he and his team are providing or working on has the highest quality. A manager is also responsible for getting the work out as quickly as possible, meeting due and delivery dates. If the manager's group or team falls behind, it can affect the work of other teams or departments. The third Q, quantity, means the manager has the responsibility of having his team do as much as possible to meet the department or organizational goals.

In addition, the vast majority of performance problems that a manager may encounter will stem from the 3Qs. There may be *quality* issues, such as excessive errors or mistakes by the manager's staff, or the work may not be getting done as *quickly* as it needs to, or the staff may not be doing as much as it needs to (*quantity* of work). When any of these 3Qs arise, the manager needs to give the individual staff member constructive feedback. Through constructive feedback, the problem can get resolved, allowing staff members to continue their growth and development.

The Limelight Taker: The Doris Robertson Case

Doris is the supervisor of security in a casino in the Midwest region of the country. As with all of the other accidental managers in our previous cases, Doris has had little, if any, formal training on how to manage others. Doris has been with the casino for about nine years in several different capacities. About a year ago she was moved into the security department and six months after that, when her boss left, she took over his job permanently. She was told she was "a natural" for overseeing the security staff. Doris was very surprised. She had never been in a supervisory position in any of her other jobs at the casino, and she hadn't participated in the casino's supervisory development program. All future supervisors, it seemed, went through a two-year leadership academy program before they were promoted into leadership roles. Doris began to believe that she must be a really good employee to be given this promotion—and 30 percent pay increase—especially without having to participate in the academy. (Actually, the casino needed a woman in the security supervisor position, for affirmative action reasons. There were no female candidates who had any security experience besides Doris.)

> *Symptoms of the Limelight Taker.* Limelight Takers like to be the center of attention in their groups and enjoy taking all of the credit for the good work or the success of their function, unit, or department. They seldom give credit to an employee for coming up with a creative strategy, for being a highly consistent performer, or for doing something special or out of the ordinary. They brag to other departments or upper management on how well

their group is doing because of them. They tell their own employees that the unit or department could not run without their supervision and that they, the employees, are lucky to have such a great leader. Limelight Takers go to every organizational meeting and make every presentation; they tend not to give recognition to their employees. They want everyone in the company to believe that disaster would occur if it weren't for them.

Impact on Staff. Staff members resent the Limelight Taker, whether it is their boss or one of their colleagues. They believe if they have done something well they should get the credit for it. They also appropriately believe that no one person is responsible for the success of any team. Because this resentment builds up over time, eventually the staff will lose respect for the Limelight Taker. They also become angry and demoralized and attempt to undermine the credibility of the Limelight Taker. They know what is going on and want everyone else in the organization to realize it as well.

Impact on Department/Organization. When employees are victims of a Limelight Taker, they will do whatever is necessary to demonstrate that credit is being stolen from them. This consumes much of their energy. Additionally, their anger extends beyond the individual Limelight Taker to the entire department or organization. They get distressed that other managers do not see what's really going on. A resulting consequence can be disillusionment with the entire organization and a loss of loyalty.

Why Accidental Managers Become Limelight Takers. Accidental managers are often given a story that they are the only ones who can take on a particular managerial role, that the company desperately needs them, and that they are exceptional in their line of work. This is done to convince them to become the manager (there are some accidental managers, though a small percentage, for whom the story is true). They are put on a pedestal and start to believe that they belong there, no matter what they do. Before long, they can develop the "big head" syndrome. Power corrupts and is an aphrodisiac.

Hints for the Limelight Taker. Becoming a good manager, accidental or not, takes times and much hard work. But it is a very rewarding experience when successful. One of the keys to managerial success is being able to rely on your staff to help you accomplish your department's objectives. Develop staff members by training them and delegating to them. Work with them. You need them. Give them the recognition that they deserve. Share the limelight with them.

The Self-Castigator: The Henry Okum Case

Henry is a manager in the purchasing department of a Fortune 500 company in Chicago. He took on one of the managerial slots over ten months ago. He was told that it would be a temporary assignment. Henry agreed to the shift in responsibilities because he was asked to do so by his VP. Henry had never met or spoken to the VP before that time. The VP told Henry that he was highly respected among his colleagues for doing good work and that they needed someone for a few weeks to supervise the nineteen-member group (the group that he was now part of.) It was something Henry didn't want to do, but he was not about to refute the VP. A few weeks turned into almost one year as the company was forced to put a hiring freeze into effect about a week after Henry took on his managerial duties.

Henry doesn't like to complain and is a real company man. He has asked his boss, the director of the department, when this temporary assignment would be over. The boss told him to hang in there. Henry has no complaints about his subordinates. They are knowledgeable and hardworking for the most part. It is just that he isn't comfortable in his current role. He feels he does not have the personality to manage. However, his subordinates, when they are asked, say that Henry is doing fine.

Henry finds the interaction with people—coaching, performance reviews, counseling, reviewing standards and objectives, staff meetings and lunches, etc.—extremely stressful for him. But he won't directly ask for help and instead bears the brunt of every situation.

Symptoms of the Self-Castigator. Self-Castigators tend to have low self-esteem and get very upset with themselves. They find fault with their own work performance and criticize themselves. They say things like, "What's wrong with you? You should have known better" or "You idiot, why did you do it that way?" On paper, they are doing well on the job, but they never perceive it that way. When a subordinate makes a mistake, a report is late, there has been a conflict with another department, or a customer complains, the Self-Castigator will take the blame.

Impact on Staff. Staff members usually feel sorry for the Self-Castigator. They cannot understand why the Self-Castigator manager constantly blames himself or herself for things that were the fault of others or the fault of no one. Many staff members will try to understand the behavior of the Self-Castigator. If they are unable to do so, the work environment becomes less pleasant and negativity increases as Self-Castigators begin to affect the moods of other people in their departments.

Impact on Department/Organization. Because it is an unpleasant experience being with the Self-Castigator, eventually departmental staff will try to avoid this person. (This avoidance only feeds the Self-Castigator's doubts about his performance.) When people avoid their boss, communication suffers; less information is shared; and there are fewer opportunities to discuss problems, concerns, and solutions. All of these behaviors impact the bottom lines of productivity and profitability.

Why Accidental Managers Become Self-Castigators. Often people put into new situations with little experience or preparation doubt that they can be successful. Their doubt doubles or triples when they are put in these situations against their will. Also, individuals become Self-Castigators to express their need for help or to let others know they are very uncomfortable doing what they are doing—they are practically screaming, "Get me out of here!"

Hints for the Self-Castigator. Don't be afraid to speak up and ask for help. People will respect their manager more for that and feel that he is concerned about succeeding. The best way for Self-Castigator managers (or any manager from our worst list) to change their behavior is to identify the specific behaviors they would like to change and the alternative behaviors to take their place. Then the manager must practice the new behaviors until he becomes comfortable with them. Eventually that new behavior will replace the old one until it becomes the new habit. To facilitate this process, the manager needs to identify one or more individuals he trusts who can give him honest feedback on how he's doing. For example, if I am a Self-Castigating manager and I want to stop blaming myself for the mistakes that others make and put the blame where it belongs, I need to tell someone what behavior I want to change. That person should be able to observe me in the workplace and give me feedback if I am doing less of the old behavior and more of the new one.

Additionally, Self-Castigators should realize how their actions affect others, especially those on their staff. Staff members may lose their own self-confidence when they are around managers who are continually criticizing themselves. Self-castigating behavior is the type of behavior staff doesn't expect or accept from someone in a leadership role.

The Waffler: The Mike Lyn Case

Mike was elated when he got word that he was being promoted to manager at one of the largest pharmaceutical companies in the world. Until then, he hadn't given promotional opportunities much thought because it is very difficult to move up within his company. Besides, he was very happy doing his cancer research. But Mike knew that with this promotion, he would have more opportunity to interface with managers from other laboratories and learn more about research projects they are engaged in. He was also in a much better position to advocate for more funds from senior management for the research projects his laboratory handles. Mike's only concern about this new opportunity was that he found it very hard to make decisions, and he knew that managers had to make difficult decisions and sometimes very fast decisions as well. All in all, Mike was quite happy with the sudden turn of events and was looking forward to his new job.

> *Symptoms of the Waffler.* The Waffler procrastinates in making decisions. He is always thinking of all the possible options that he has or is looking for more data or information. He often goes around telling others that he has to make a decision and asks for their opinions. Or he just busies himself with other projects or work in order to avoid having to make the decision.
>
> *Impact on Staff.* Staff members do not like to work for managers who are indecisive. In fact, when you ask employees what they dislike about their bosses the most, indecisiveness tends to be on the top of the list. When managers vacillate, their interests, as employees, are being neglected. They also assume that their manager doesn't know what she is really doing.
>
> *Impact on Department/Organization.* Often decisions need to be

made quickly by the person in charge. You cannot always involve your staff in helping you make the decision or have the luxury of asking others within or outside the organization for their thoughts. Opportunities are lost that may never reappear when decisions are not made in a timely manner or not made at all.

Why Accidental Managers Become Wafflers. Wafflers are fearful that they will make the wrong decision and that making a wrong decision is a direct reflection on their abilities. They also believe if they can procrastinate in making a decision, its importance will diminish and they will be off the hook. Many managers are thrown into the role of decision maker without being ready for it. Decision making is a skill that many managers have not had much experience with, nor have they received the necessary training.

Hints for the Waffler. Indecisive managers need to recognize first and foremost that delayed decision making, or non–decision making, will have an impact on the overall goals of the organization. They must set strict decision-making deadlines for themselves. They need to share with others the decision that needs to be made and on what date. Then they need these other people to hold them accountable for making a decision by the deadline. Eventually, Wafflers will learn to hold themselves accountable for decision making and decision-making deadlines.

The Braggart: The Alana Jones Case

Alana has received several awards from professional organizations in her field. She is a well-known chemist and has published many articles. When she was asked to take on a managerial role, she had no qualms about it. She knew she would be great at it and it would just be another way for her to showcase her many talents. The only thing she objected to was the people she would have to manage. They did not know nearly as much as she did, nor would they ever.

Symptoms of the Braggart. People like Alana will tell anyone who asks (and many who do not ask) how good they are in anything that they put their hands to. There are genuine braggarts. That is, people who do in fact know quite a bit and are entitled to some bragging rights. And then there are the types who "think they know it all" and go around telling everyone how great they are when, in reality, they aren't. Braggarts, of either type, find any opportunity to brag. It could be while they are at a team meeting, communicating with an individual team member, on the phone with a customer, or at the car wash.

Impact on Staff. Even though most staff members like to work for people who are bright and recognized in their field, they still look to their manager for positive feedback and recognition. They also look to their manager to train and support them. Braggarts don't do this, and it is very demoralizing to the staff members.

Impact on Department/Organization. Organizations like it when they have an employee who is well known in her field and is an expert. However, when that person is in a managerial role she needs to do what all other managers do—that is, lead and manage. When that does not occur, the organization suffers.

Why Accidental Managers Become Braggarts. There are many accidental managers who deep down feel that managing is beneath them. They also do not want to have to associate with individuals such as their team members who are less skilled or qualified than they are. To compensate for that, they overly exaggerate their technical abilities or their past performances in order to get their team members to respect them.

Hints for the Braggart. The Braggart manager has to let her excellent work performance and high level of skill speak for itself. There is no need to continually tell others about your accomplishments. Doing this actually gets others to think much less of you and your achievements. Braggarts have to get down to the business of managing and come to realize that it is their role to develop their team members. They also need to have the belief that most team members have the ability to succeed at high levels of performance.

The Deceiver: The Alan Sanchez Case

Alan manages a group of five copyeditors. He promised Dillon, one of the editors, that he would be sent to the annual editors' convention if he kept performing at his current high level. He also told Dillon that he would be rated in the top category of the company's performance review system and would be the first in line for promotion to senior copyeditor. Dillon was told all of this in the last four months. None of these promises were kept. Alan deceived Dillon. Dillon did not get to go to the convention, he was rated in the average category, and someone else got the promotion.

Symptoms of the Deceiver. Deceivers do not tell the truth. They lie, embellish the truth, or make up stories. They deceive others because they do not want to recognize what is really happening, or they don't know what is really happening and need to respond in some way, or they like to see the strong emotional reactions, positive or negative, of others.

Impact on Staff. People have a tremendous dislike for being lied to, even if it was unintentional or there was no malice intended. Deception is near the top of the list of reasons managers lose the trust and loyalty of their staff. It is impossible for people to have a constructive working relationship with a manager who deceives them.

Impact on Department/Organization. For organizations to succeed, staff members need to be working toward their goals in a supportive work environment. When individuals are deceived by their managers, goals lose their relevance and the environment becomes destructive. When this occurs, the quality of performance and output suffers.

Why Accidental Managers Become Deceivers. Accidental managers often don't have the information they need. They do not know where to get it or whom to ask for it. They don't want to come across as looking unprepared or uninformed to their team members, so they make up the facts.

Hints for the Deceiver. Managers are much more respected and liked when they tell the truth, even if the truth is unpleasant at first. It is better to tell someone that he's being sent to another department than to tell him that he's not being affected by a reorganization. Eventually team members will find out that a manager has lied, and then the relationship is destroyed. If a manager has "accidentally" deceived a team member, she must, as soon as possible, admit that she did so. If she does that, it is still possible that the relationship can be held intact.

The Exaggerator Congratulator: The Gary Prince Case

Gary got the word only yesterday that he was taking over as the manager of the parks and recreation department. Gary worked in city government for a medium-size city near New Orleans. He didn't know anything about managing, just what he had learned from the managers he had worked for, whose styles he definitely didn't like. They were directive and micromanaged. They wouldn't hassle you as long as you did what they said. If you did not, they would blow up. After working with those types of managers, Gary figured that the best thing for him to do as a manager was to make everyone happy: staff, colleagues, bosses, and the community that uses the parks and recreational areas that he was now in charge of. Life was too short to take things so seriously.

Symptoms of the Exaggerator Congratulator. These managers go around praising everyone they come in contact with, using grandiose terminology. They tell their staff members that they are doing the greatest work imaginable, that they are the best staff ever. The boss is told that she is the best boss since the creation of bosses. Customers hear that their children are the brightest, the best athletes, the best looking, etc. If permitted to, these managers write glowing performance reviews and want to place everyone in the "walks on water" category. They tend to overlook or minimize problems and to laugh things off. They seem to be genuinely happy, and to them the world seems perfect.

Impact on Staff. The vast majority of team members, at first, would relish the chance to work for this type of boss. It would be fun, their egos would rise, and it would be quite a change from many of the managers who they are used to working with. Then again, over time they would find out how disingenuous the Exaggerator Congratulator boss really is. They would become disillusioned and start to feel that the boss really wasn't a support system for them. They would discount the exaggerated praise and lip service and lose their respect and confidence in the boss. Most team members would eventually view him as a joke.

Impact on Department/Organization. The Exaggerator Congratulator's behavior soon backfires on him. He's discounted as an effective manager and, once again, as we have seen with so many other worst types of managers, the morale of the department starts to decrease, resulting in lower productivity and lessening of work quality.

Why Accidental Managers Become Exaggerator Congratulators. Some managers who become Exaggerator Congratulators feel that the major responsibility of a manager is public relations. They think that as long as everyone appears to be happy, the organization will believe that their unit or department is running smoothly. Other managers who become this type of worst manager just don't want to take the job of managing seriously and give it the attention that it demands.

Hints for the Exaggerator Congratulator. Giving praise is great, but Exaggerator Congratulators do not give it the way it should be given. Praise must be genuine and sincere. It also needs to be specific, not vague or general. Exaggerator Congratulators need to stop the bull and get down to business. They need to do all the other things that successful managers do: set goals and standards, monitor performance, train, delegate, actively listen, give constructive feedback, etc. An Exaggerator Congratulator will fool some of the people some of the time. Everyone else will pick up on his insincere praise very quickly.

Chapter Summary

These ten types of worst managers exist in many organizations, and accidental managers often turn into them if they are not careful or aware of their own behavior. These worst types of managers diminish the success of their staff and, ultimately, the success of their departments and organizations. By learning the "do nothing" approach (Chapter 3) and using the Platinum skills that enable managers to do nothing (Chapters 4–7), managers can stop themselves from turning into any one of these All-Time Worst Manager types.

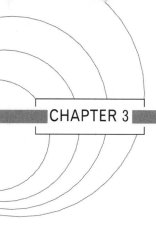

The Key to Success: "Doing Nothing"

To obtain value from this chapter and the rest of this book, accidental managers need to be in the mind-set that they are committed to trying to succeed in the managerial role. The commitment and interest need to be high to give managing an all-out try. (Keep in mind, once again, that the accidental manager always has the option of declining the managerial career path and the potentially rewarding opportunity it represents.) In this chapter, the "do nothing" approach to managing is defined and described, including the benefits of "doing nothing," why some managers avoid "doing nothing," and when it's not appropriate to "do nothing." The last section of the chapter gives advice on how to get started on the road to managing successfully.

The "Do Nothing" Approach

How do you avoid becoming one of the ten All-Time Worst Manager types and succeed at managing? Let's explore some ideas.

Think about your current management job. Make a list of everything that takes up your time at work during any given week.

My List:

_____   _____

_____   _____

_____   _____

_____   _____

_____   _____

_____   _____

Before we come back to this list, let's define a few terms first.

- ✔ *Doing.* Doing is working on a specific goal on your own, starting and completing some type of work on your own, or taking something from input to output. Examples of "doing" behavior include preparing the budget, developing slides for a presentation, making the presentation, developing a new formula, coming up with new procedures, compiling time sheets, completing status reports, responding to customer complaints, or searching for a vendor to provide some management training for your organization.

- ✔ *Managing.* Managing is getting the work done through others by having them help you achieve the goals of the unit, department, or organization. Examples of managing include planning the work (what has to get done), organizing it (who does what), communicating it (training, giving directions, explaining procedures), monitoring (making sure the work is getting done), and evaluating (assessing how well the work was accomplished). More specific managerial competencies include interviewing and selecting new team members, managing the budget and resources, disciplining, correcting performance, holding regularly scheduled coaching and performance review sessions, resolving conflicts, determining success measures, working with individual team members to assess their level of skills and knowledge, and correcting mistakes and errors.

- ✔ *Leading.* Leading is getting people to willingly do their jobs by providing the right type of personal environment for people to want to succeed. Examples include listening to individuals, encouraging and motivating them to perform at their highest levels, giving them praise and recognition, showing support, telling them why their jobs are important, being the role model, encouraging change, being persistent and not giving up easily, sharing and communicating the unit's or department's vision, and being proactive in promoting communication among team members and between the team and other groups.

All three of these behaviors—doing, managing, and leading—are crucial for the success of the vast majority of organizations. One behavior is not more important than the others. In most companies, in general, as you ascend the first few rungs of the management hierarchy, "doing" decreases and managing and leading behaviors increase. As you reach the top of the hierarchy (e.g., becoming a CEO, VP, or director), leading behavior increases and managing behavior decreases.

I like the way Peter Senge, an expert in management and leadership development, distinguishes between managing and leading. He says that the manager's job is to solve problems and the leader's job is to create them (just a bit of humor here). Actually, Senge says the leader's job is to *create solutions*. At first, these definitions may sound quite similar, but they are quite different. Managing is more reactive and more operational, happening day to day. Leadership is more proactive and future oriented. Organizations need both behaviors to do well.

Now, go back to the list you created. Review each item and decide whether it is more of a doing, managing, or leading behavior. Sometimes behaviors can cross categories. For example, running a meeting can cover all three behaviors. It is "doing" because you are the one running the meeting. It is "managing" because at the meeting you are planning and organizing work. It is "leading" because you are motivating and encouraging your team to succeed.

What did you discover? Hopefully you listed many items that fall in the managing and leading categories. The more responsibilities you have that fall in these two categories, the more you will succeed as a manager and be happy and successful in that role. Your goal, even though it may not be your reality today, is to spend as much of your day as possible managing and leading. Your goal is to *do nothing*!

Let me explain further. When I say "do nothing," I don't mean that successful managers spend their day golfing or surfing the Net or writing their resume for their next job. *If managers are doing nothing it means they are spending their days managing and leading.* They are not doing the work themselves. This is what the best managers try to do. The whole idea of managing successfully is to get as much of the work as possible done through your team and for you to get your team to want to do it. Everyone wins with this approach.

No matter how high they reach in the management chain, managers are always "doing." Managers always have their own work responsibilities. Managers need to make presentations at meetings, respond to client complaints, work on projects where they have the experience and expertise, do strategic planning, interview, and take clients out to lunch.

However, managers succeed or become successful in their managerial roles by developing their team members to do the doing. They train and delegate tasks to those on their team, actively listening, giving and receiving feedback, and motivating their team members. If managers do their managerial job (managing and leading their team), they can do less of the doing. They can spend more time managing and leading because their team is now able to do more of the day-to-day work on its own.

Benefits of Doing Nothing

The manager, the staff members, and the department (or organization) all benefit from the "do nothing" approach in the following ways:

✔ *The manager has more time.* Once managers learn to develop their staff by determining what productivity stage different staff members are at, and then train them and delegate to them (Chapter 4), the staff will be able to take on more of the daily responsibilities and assignments. This frees up the manager to spend more time managing and leading, or to work on projects that the manager didn't have time for before, whether it is getting a hand back into work that the manager misses or taking on new projects from above. Most accidental managers, after investing time to manage and lead and develop their staff, find the management job to be interesting, fun, challenging, and rewarding.

✔ *The staff has more opportunities for growth and development.* When a manager "does nothing" (i.e., manages and leads more), the manager allows the staff opportunities to develop new skills and abilities, as well as to learn more about how the group or department functions. Additionally, the motivational level of staff members increases because of their increased visibility in the department and new decision-making authority. Many employees I have worked with who initially resisted these additional "opportunities" now tell me they feel so much better about their capabilities, and more marketable! And in today's work environment that is about the best feeling to have.

✔ *The organization strengthens the work unit.* The organization will have more individuals who know how to do more. This increases the organization's wealth. An organization's biggest equity (its staff) will be "worth" so much more. To emphasize this point, let me share this brief true story.

The Intranet Case

A few years ago I was consulting in the largest utility company in southern California. I was working in one of the larger departments, the business group developing a management-training program. This department had about 300 employees with its own intranet. Shelia, the manager who ran the system, was very bright and thoroughly knowledgeable about the system. In fact, there were a few features of the system that only she had expertise on. They were her favorite features and she enjoyed working on them herself. She did all the doing and didn't allow any of her staff to manage these features.

One day she got a call from an Internet start-up firm in Seattle. The firm offered her twice her current salary, a one-year housing relocation bonus, and a guaranteed three-year contract. But she was told she had to start immediately, literally within a few days. The same day that she got this incredible offer she went to see the department head and gave notice. The boss begged her to stay and offered her a raise and new office, but Shelia declined and exited the building within the hour. The irony is that this utility company had to hire Shelia back as a consultant, on weekends, at an exorbitant fee, to train a few of her former staff members how to run those features of the system that previously only she had assumed responsibility for. Shelia, and the department, hadn't built up their equity. That is, they were not developing other staff members to learn the skills that Shelia had. I was personally irked by this story because, as an end user of this utility company, I and other end users were indirectly billed for the training costs involved.

Managerial Excuses for Not "Doing Nothing"

"Doing nothing" seems to be beneficial to all parties involved. If that is true, then why are so many managers not "doing nothing?" There are four main excuses that managers have for not "doing nothing." Let's look at the excuses and explain why each of these excuses doesn't hold much logic.

1. *"Don't Have the Time."* Many managers say they just do not have the time to develop, listen to, give feedback to, or motivate their staff. They are too busy doing. They believe they would never be able to get everything done if they had to spend time managing and leading. They pretty much leave their team alone, step in when there are problems or emergencies, and hope for the best.

   The Counter-Argument: It is true that managing and leading take a lot of time. In reality, they should take most of a manager's time. But the more managers manage and lead, the more time they will have in the future because their team members will be able to do more and more on their own and take over much of the work that the manager currently has to do herself.

2. *Omnipotence.* Some managers hold the perception that they can do their assignments better and faster than any employee ever could. This perception is reinforced when they are told that this is the reason they got the managerial job in the first place.

The Counter-Argument: These managers may be right in their belief that they can currently perform a job better than anyone else. But if they try to do everything themselves, they will eventually burn out and turn into drowning workaholics. Many managers are guilty of omnipotence. They feel that they are the only ones who can do things well. This is a fallacy. There is probably someone out there who, with some training and direction, can do a task as well, maybe even better. If a manager believes she is the only one who can do something so well, then she will become the only one doing it. And eventually, if she doesn't trust others enough to try to teach them how to do a task better, she will be the one doing everything.

3. *Overloading*. Many accidental managers know that their employees are already too busy. They do not want to overload them even more by offloading additional work to them.

   The Counter-Argument: This is a very powerful concern. However, if the manager had more time to manage and lead, he could reexamine his employees' priorities and how they use their time, and then train and develop them so they could do more by working differently. Many managers also make the false assumption that they can only "do nothing" if they have employees who are performing at the highest levels. The more competent employee, who has demonstrated dependable performance over time, is obviously the best candidate for delegating work to. But managers must be careful not to select these individuals too often or exclusively because that will end up overburdening a few people. In addition, others may interpret this as favoritism. Keep in mind that you can exert management/leadership behavior by developing your less competent employees, making them more competent so they can assume more responsibilities. It is even possible to get your problem or difficult employees to take on more responsibility. These individuals may be bored, frustrated, or seeking attention. Greater challenges or additional responsibilities may cause them to change their outlook and improve their performance.

4. *Company Culture*. It is the philosophy and practice in many companies that each person, even a manager, has individual assignments for which that person is solely responsible. Additionally, many companies and senior managers do not

believe in, or are not educated about, the "do nothing" approach.

The Counter-Argument: This is probably the strongest reason for not "doing nothing." However, it is up to you, as a manager, to convince upper management how the department or organization will benefit from the "do nothing" approach (although clearly it would be beneficial if upper management recognized this on its own). Many successful managers have told me that when they put their argument for doing nothing into business terms (e.g., increased productivity and profits, higher morale), their management listened and allowed them to try the "do nothing" philosophy.

Exceptions to the "Do Nothing" Rule

It is very important to point out that there are certain exceptions to the "do nothing" rule. That is, there are certain responsibilities that the manager has and should never delegate to someone else. These exceptions apply to anyone supervising others, even the CEO of an organization. These exceptions are:

✔ *Performance, salary, and quarterly reviews; disciplinary action; and coaching.* These are what we call the *personnel* responsibilities. If you have others take these on for you, there is no reason to have your position in the organizational hierarchy. For example, you do not want to say to one of your employees, "Sue is at it again. Go talk to her for me. I just cannot deal with her." These responsibilities define the core relationship of anyone managing others. Do not confuse these personnel concerns with the *personal* concerns. These occur when staff members come to you with personal problems that they are having outside of work but that are affecting their on-the-job performance. When this happens, you need to listen and be supportive but not tell the person what to do or give your personal advice. Or you can refer them to others who are qualified to handle these issues, such as the human resources department or an employee assistance program (EAP). As a manager, you are not qualified to give personal advice, and in most states you may run into legal complications if you do. As an example, let me share a case that occurred while I was consulting at a computer-parts manufacturing company in North Carolina.

The Case of the Day Care Center

A long-term and excellent employee was late two to three times a week. The supervisor spoke to her about her lateness and reminded her of the goal to be at work on time, each day. When the employee was late, it slowed down the production line. The employee apologized and explained that the day care center where she sends her child didn't open on time. She told her supervisor that she could not just leave her child there and come to work. It wasn't safe. The supervisor said that the day care center where she sends her children opened one hour earlier, and advised the employee to switch day care centers. The employee took the advice. But something very unfortunate happened to the employee's child at the new day care center. On legal counsel, the employee sued the company for "bad advice" and won. The court ruled that a supervisor, who is a representative of the company, is not qualified to give personal advice to employees.

✔ *Anything of a very sensitive or secure nature.* Often organizations want only a few people to know about certain practices. For example, there may be an impending downsizing that you are responsible for planning and implementing that the executive staff doesn't want anyone else to know about at this time.

✔ *Spending over a certain dollar limit.* Organizations have certain criteria for who can spend what. Often it has to do with your title. For example, I once worked at one of the divisions of American Express and a manager wanted to delegate a project to one of his employees. The manager believed he had developed the employee to the point where the employee was just as capable as he was of doing a very good job. He asked this employee to select and purchase software programs for the department. The employee did so. The boss got in trouble because he was the only one in the department who could sign off on purchases of more than $500.

How to Get Started on the Road to Managing Successfully

There are innumerable management and leadership skills that will help managers "do nothing." However, the ones selected in this book enable the shift of focus from doing to managing and leading to occur quickly, with the greatest impact on successful management. I call these crucial management and leadership skills the Platinum skills (see Figure 3-1). They are:

- ✔ Developing your staff, which includes training and delegating (Chapter 4)
- ✔ Active listening (Chapter 5)
- ✔ Giving and receiving feedback (Chapter 6)
- ✔ Motivating your staff (Chapter 7)

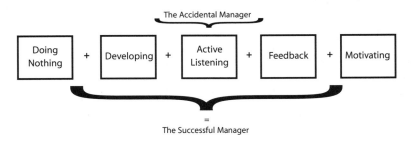

Figure 3-1. Platinum skills of managing and leading.

Another way to get started down this road to management success is to try to enjoy the job of managing and the positive effect that you can have on others. Why not make the best of being a manager? Many accidental managers have discovered that if they begin to enjoy the job and realize the important impact that they could have, everything else falls into place. Those who have taken this road tell me that it made their jobs so much easier and less stressful, and they got the results they wanted much faster than they ever thought they would. Let me share some of the tips others have shared with me that helped make them successful managers.

Get Rid of Excuses

Successful managers learn to stop blaming the company or senior management for putting them in the management position. They also stop blaming themselves for not being prepared or automatically good at managing. And they accept the fact that they may have inherited miserable staff members. They also put their energy into managing. Once they do that, the job becomes challenging and fun. Successful managers decide not to waste their creative energy on excuse making.

Try Something New

Successful managers will try something that they never thought they would do, or something that no other manager they knew of ever did before. As an example, a manager at a governmental agency in Washington, D.C. told me that she would begin each meeting with a management-related joke (a very good one, of course). It set a very different tone and built immediate rapport with the staff. Trying something new got her that home run.

Give Yourself a Big Pat on the Back

Successful managers tell themselves what they did well lately, where they have made progress, and what obstacles they overcame. They use a lot of positive self-talk. They congratulate themselves. They realize that nobody else might give them the positive feedback that they need. Then they go out and earn themselves another pat on the back. They believe in themselves.

Use Visualization

Successful managers have a picture of what they want to accomplish (e.g., establishing a good relationship with each employee, making each employee more productive), and in their minds they repeat that visual image often until it becomes part of how they view themselves and their actions. Visualizing positive pictures in their minds provides them with unexpected positive results.

Use Small Wins to Build Confidence in Your Team

Successful managers recognize their team members for incremental improvements or whenever they finish or accomplish part of an assignment or project. Waiting until the end to express gratitude doesn't work as well.

Speak with Passion, Demonstrate Your Commitment

Successful managers get excited when results are achieved. They are enthusiastic when assigning tasks or projects. They don't give up, and they encourage others to try their hardest.

Communicate the Vision Constantly

When managers share information about customers, the business environment, what's happening in the department, the company's future direction, etc., their team members usually become much more interested in the work they are doing. They are better able to see the connection between their tasks and the goals of the department and organization.

Let Your Intentions Be Known

Hopefully, managers have good intentions. They want to manage well and have their team succeed. However, having good intentions is not enough because no one really knows what managers' good intentions are. What managers get judged on in the workplace are their actions, behaviors, and the results they achieve. Successful managers know that they have to put their good intentions into practice, not just keep them to themselves.

Foster Self-Reliance

Some managers believe that being there to help out employees is the best thing a manager can do. It shows interest and concern and earns employees' respect. Actually, many successful managers learn quite the opposite. They come to realize that, in most instances, if they encourage their employees to learn, develop, and work more independently (and interdependently with other employees), they will feel much better about themselves and the quality, quantity, and speed of their work will improve. One of the best methods for fostering self-reliance is to involve team members in decision making. When staff members are involved in decision making, or make decisions on their own, they are much more likely to believe in the decision and implement it than if the manager made the decision on her own. When successful managers involve their team members in the decision-making process, their team members "own" the decision.

Get a Mentor

The best organizations provide a mentor for managers to help them learn the culture, politics, and accepted managerial practices of the organization. If the organization doesn't provide a mentor, then successful managers, when they have to, find their own mentors. The manager has to find someone in the organization that she and everyone else on her team respects and whom she believes is an excellent manager. Then she has to ask the individual if he would be willing to help out her and her team.

Build Trust and Believability

Early in their tenures, managers discover that if their staff trusts and believes them, that makes the job of managing so much easier and they are likely to be much more successful. Building trust and believability is not easy because most employees are somewhat suspicious of the motivations of their managers. But, if managers do what they say, carry through on promises, advocate for their staff, tell the truth, provide necessary material and people resources, communicate continually, get to know each staff member on an individual basis, and provide opportunities for staff to develop and grow, then chances are high that trust will be established.

Chapter Summary

The "do nothing" philosophy of successful management is an approach recommended for anyone in management. There are differences among doing, managing, and leading, and a manager's goal should be to do as much managing and leading as possible. Managers have excuses for not wanting to "do nothing" and there are arguments to counter those excuses. On the other hand, there are legitimate exceptions for *not* "doing nothing." The suggestions offered by former accidental managers who have learned to accept and enjoy the managerial job can help you, too, become successful at managing.

CHAPTER 4

The Platinum Skill of Developing Your Team Members

The first of the Platinum skills for becoming a successful manager is developing others. Developing means determining and clearly describing and defining the productivity stage of each of your team members based on their action and behaviors, then giving them resources, support, guidance, supervision, and the feedback they need for that stage. The ultimate goal of developing others is to get them to work as independently and interdependently as possible— having them do the doing. Often new managers tend to rescue their people instead. They do the work for them, make all the decisions, or leave employees at their current level of satisfactory or below-par performance. By rescuing, managers are not developing their employees, and so they are undermining the "do nothing" approach. This chapter looks at the five productivity stages of employee performance and describes what actions a manager needs to take for individuals within each of these stages in order to develop them further. The chapter concludes by focusing on two important supportive skills for development of team members: training and delegating.

Productivity Stages

Figure 4-1 indicates the correlation between productivity stage and doing behavior. There are five productivity stages:

Stage 1: Attention Getting
Stage 2: Flying Blind
Stage 3: Steadiness
Stage 4: On the Rise
Stage 5: Doing

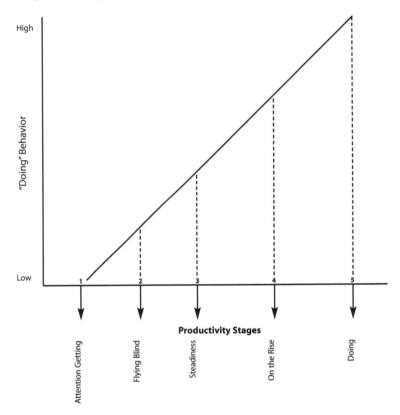

Figure 4-1. Productivity stages and "doing" behavior.

The higher the stage a team member is at, the more she can "do" and the more the manager can "do nothing." If managers can have 80 percent of their team members at stages 4 and 5, they will have an easier time managing and become more successful and effective at managing. The best accidental managers—indeed the best managers—strive to develop employees at the highest productivity stages. In fact, I would surmise that in the more profitable and productive companies in the world—for example, those that receive Malcolm Baldrige awards for excellence yearly, such as Microsoft, 3M,

Southwest Airlines, and SAS—more than 80 percent of staff members are performing at either productivity stage 4 or 5.

An employee can begin at any productivity stage. A new employee, for example, does not have to begin at stage 1. She can come into the organization already performing at stage 4. Individuals can continually shift among these stages. Your better managers rarely have staff members "shifting downward." They are continually trying to develop their people. Additionally, individuals do not necessarily develop stage by stage. There are countless examples of employees jumping stages, going from the "flying blind" stage to the "on the rise" stage very quickly, bypassing the "steadiness" stage.

Let's look at each productivity stage in more detail. In each case we'll:

✔ Describe the behaviors and actions associated with the productivity stage.

✔ Provide one or more concrete illustrations.

✔ Delineate the actions an effective manager needs to take with a team member who is at that stage.

Please note that in any of these stages an employee usually does not exhibit all of the behaviors/actions associated with that stage. Also, even though managers associate employees with a particular stage, they can have some of the behaviors/actions of the other stages as well.

Stage 1: Attention Getting

In this stage the employee is not fully participating in the success of the organization. He has performance issues or habits that negatively impact his success, the success of others, or the success of the organization. His "doing" behavior is low.

Behaviors/Actions

✔ Lacks knowledge about how to do the job

✔ Makes many mistakes

✔ Misses deadlines

- ✓ Outputs minimal work (e.g., low quantity)
- ✓ Abuses time excessively (e.g., late, absent, missing in action)
- ✓ Doesn't follow set procedures
- ✓ Doesn't share information
- ✓ Violates organizational rules
- ✓ Impacts the productivity of others through poor performance or poor workplace attitude
- ✓ Displays inappropriate dress, language, or appearance
- ✓ Socializes excessively (e.g., abuses telephone or Internet access privileges)
- ✓ Doesn't follow safety rules or regulations, thereby putting herself or others at risk

Illustration A: The Mechanical Engineer

Ken works in the design department of an automotive manufacturing company in Great Britain. He is a mechanical engineer with responsibility for designing computer sketches for certain engine parts. He is in a unit with three other mechanical engineers who have responsibilities for other engine parts. Their ultimate goal is to turn their sketches over to the engine construction division. Ken never completes his assignments on time, thus causing serious delays in the production schedule.

Managerial Action A

The manager needs to find out why Ken is missing these deadlines. Is it because he isn't aware of the deadlines, or is there some conflict with his team members? Or perhaps he isn't skilled enough to complete the sketches on time. Depending on the cause, the managerial actions may differ. They could involve information sharing about dates and deadlines, conflict resolution, or training. Communicating the problem and listening to the employee's issues is critical.

Illustration B: Wrong Information

Charles works the help desk for a small Internet provider firm in the South. When clients call with technical issues, he sometimes gives them the wrong information. This leads to the clients having to call again to complain and asking to speak to another technician. The reputation of this Internet provider suffers as a result of Charles's actions.

Managerial Action B

Similar to the managerial action given in Illustration A, the manager has to determine if this is a skill or attitude issue. Does Charles lack technical knowledge, or for some reason is he purposely giving incorrect responses? If it is the former, training is required. If it is the latter, counseling is needed.

Illustration C: The Assembly Line

Leanne works the assembly line for a beverage firm. She is often absent and does not call in until well after her shift has begun. She has been coached, counseled, and reprimanded for this many times before. Leanne's behavior causes a major halt in production until the supervisor can find a replacement for her.

Managerial Action C

The manager needs to follow the company's discipline procedure, which could include issuing written and oral warnings, notifying the human resources department and the union representative, developing action plans for improvement, following up on any improvements, and pointing out the negative consequences of failure to improve. If all of these steps do not bring a positive change in the performance or the behavior of the staff member, termination may be necessary.

All of the managerial actions for the attention-getting productivity stage involve training or feedback to improve the team member's performance or behavior, transferring the team member to a different department for a better job fit, or taking disciplinary action. If these actions are not taken, the employee will continue to perform at these same low levels or cause others to perform at lower levels than their norm. If the manager does not step in, stage 1 team members will never reach stage 5 productivity, where the manager can have them doing specified tasks. If the manager does not take action the team member will get the message that his performance or behavior is acceptable. Many team members do not even know that they have issues of concern until they are told. They must be given the feedback and held accountable for change. It is possible that employees who have inappropriate habits or behaviors may still be performing adequately or even well. Nevertheless, they are still considered to be in productivity stage 1 because their behaviors or habits will eventually impact their performance or the performance of others, or go against company rules, regulations, or procedures. From my experience, about 97 percent of individual staff members experiencing behavior problems or displaying inappropriate habits have an impact on productivity and/or profitability.

Stage 2: Flying Blind

In this productivity stage the employee is very motivated to do a good job and tries very hard to succeed. However, he does not have the skills, knowledge, or training to perform well on his own. If we leave him alone, he will make major mistakes and probably become less motivated.

Behaviors/Actions
- Keeps busy all of the time
- Has high energy
- Displays positive attitude
- Feels embarrassed or fearful of admitting weaknesses
- Is unaware of skill gaps

✔ Shows willingness to help and pitch in; very cooperative

✔ Works late; doesn't take time for lunch

✔ Has lots of undiscovered mistakes

✔ Has not accomplished goals set

✔ Knows much less than is apparent

✔ Is liked by everyone

✔ Works on what he likes to work on

Illustration A: The Instructional Designer

Dottie recently graduated with an MS degree from a prestigious university on the West Coast. She landed a job as an instructional designer for new product training at an established high-tech firm. Dottie's boss was impressed with her scholastic record and the thesis Dottie had done on the flaws in a technical training program. Dottie was assigned to the training department, where her first project was to develop a two-day training program for the sales force that would be selling the firm's new products. Dottie was enthusiastic and worked diligently. When she handed in the rough sketch of the program to her boss, the boss was shocked. To her dismay, she discovered that Dottie had no clue how to design a technical training program.

Managerial Action A

The manager could have prevented Dottie from "flying blind" by monitoring Dottie's work more closely, especially at the beginning, until she sensed that Dottie could handle the project. We cannot make the assumption that just because someone had good grades and went to an excellent school, or did well in previous projects or jobs, he or she would know exactly what to do on the job. Once the manager found out that Dottie did not have the necessary skills, the manager needed to train her, guide her, supervise her closely, and support her.

Illustration B: Finding Your Own Projects

A few years ago a bad manager (one of the worst managers I have ever met) from a Fortune 100 company told me a story that illustrates what it means to be flying blind. In this company of approximately 5,000 people, it was the responsibility of each employee to find his or her own projects to get assigned to. According to this manager, it took him three years to figure out what one of his employees was up to! This would only be true of a very bad manager.

From April through January, this employee was about the busiest employee you could find. He would come in earlier than others, stay late, was continually on his PC or the phone, and was always having short meetings in the company's conference rooms. Then, for the months of February and March, this employee would sit around with not much to do until the following April, when he was as busy as before. The manager thought that anyone who seemed to be so busy must have been working very hard and probably needed a two-month break. Do you want to venture a guess what was happening in this scenario? You may not believe it, but the employee took it upon himself to set up and run both the company football and baseball pools. This became his full-time job. It involved research, preparing spreadsheets, collecting and distributing money, recruiting new customers, coaching people how to play, etc. The two months of downtime—February and March—were when no professional football or baseball games took place.

Managerial Action B

To prevent employees from languishing in the flying blind stage, managers need to know at all times what their employees are doing. They need to set goals, help employees achieve these goals through training and coaching, and then challenge them with new goals. Managers also need to have regularly scheduled reviews of each of their team member's work products.

Stage 3: Steadiness

In this stage the staff member is "doing," but only at a moderate level. Employees are often labeled as "average" performers.

Behaviors/Actions

- ✔ Comes to work regularly and usually on time
- ✔ Completes assignments and projects satisfactorily most of the time
- ✔ Performs at a moderate "doing" level
- ✔ Cooperates with other team members and is considerate and helpful
- ✔ Does not ask for additional responsibilities
- ✔ Shows little interest in advancing or developing new skills
- ✔ Does not offer ideas, opinions, or suggestions unless asked
- ✔ Does as he is told; does not disagree or express contrary opinions
- ✔ Is resistant to change; likes things as they are

Illustration A: Resistant to Development

Jamie works as an ad-space salesperson. She almost always meets her sales quotas, and clients and coworkers have pleasant things to say about her. Several people in her group with whom she started out have moved on to higher-paying jobs with more responsibility. Jamie's boss has consistently given her satisfactory performance reviews. When the boss gives her new or different work assignments, which will increase her current skill level, Jamie does them, but she doesn't seem to be too interested in or excited about these opportunities.

Managerial Action A

Steady team members cause a dilemma for most managers. They are doing their jobs, are willing to do anything else you ask them to do, get fairly good results, but are content to stay at that level. The manager has two choices here. The first is to let such employees alone and allow them to perform at their current "doing" level. After all, they are doing what's in their job descriptions and are being rated as satisfactory on performance appraisals. But a manager has to ask herself if that is acceptable to her organization. Shouldn't the manager try to get as many people as possible to productivity stages 4 and 5? If she believes the current level of performance isn't acceptable, she has a second option. The manager can explain that she is interested in further developing the steady team member and outline how she will do that. She could also point out that there will be new expectations and accountability, but the individual will benefit by moving to a higher productivity stage. Once that occurs, promotional opportunities or other benefits could arise.

Listening to team members who are at productivity stage 3 is important and appropriate because these employees may not be interested in new challenges. Perhaps it is because of a skill issue, a struggle they are having in their personal lives, or they may feel that they lack the political profile to succeed at a higher productivity stage. Managers need to assume the responsibility of finding out what the issues are and then help the team members develop, if that is the team members' choice.

Illustration B: The Silent One

James has been working with an engineering consulting firm for a little under a year. He graduated near the top of his class from one of the more prestigious universities. James's boss and owner of the firm, Timothy, was excited to get James to come to work for him. Timothy thought that it would take a few months for James to learn the way the firm operated and to become familiar with the types of projects they worked on. However, James's progress has been much slower than anticipated and this worries Timothy. The firm is one of the smaller ones and every staff member needs to produce to the fullest. Staff members are expected to go out and bring in as much business as they can on their own. Besides being engineers, they also have to be salespeople. James just doesn't seem to be that passionate or interested in what he is doing, even though Timothy knows that James has the skills and knowledge to perform his projects at the highest level. The few times that Timothy has spoken to James about his work performance James replies that he just needs some more time to become comfortable with the way the firm operates. Timothy cannot wait any longer for James to come around. He needs his energy and full-blown commitment now.

Managerial Action B

Timothy can try to continue to speak with James to find out if there are other issues causing his lackadaisical performance. If there are, Timothy can try to address them. Sometimes, however—and all managers need to recognize this—there can be a poor job fit. James may not have the personality or presence that's needed by this firm. He may not be the entrepreneurial type and may be happier in another organization. Managers need to try to determine during the recruitment and interviewing period whether a candidate's background and personality match what the organization is looking for. This doesn't always happen, and then the manager and organization need to decide what to do. They can stay with the staff member, work with him, and hope he changes, or they can realize the employee would do better elsewhere.

Stage 4: On the Rise

This is one of the productivity stages (along with productivity stage 5) that managers want as many of their staff members to aspire to. It is at this stage that staff is "performing" at moderately high or at high levels.

Behaviors/Actions

✔ Works independently with some guidance from the manager

✔ Shows interest in the job

✔ Demonstrates willingness to offer suggestions and ideas on how to improve the work

✔ Works interdependently with other staff members

✔ Produces high work quality and quantity, as a rule

✔ Wants to learn more and increase skills

✔ Feels insecure about work and abilities on occasion

✔ Has a high sense of loyalty to the organization

✔ Is very dependable and trustworthy

Illustration A: Barkley from MIS

Months ago Barkley was hired to work in the MIS department of a commercial bank in New Hampshire. He interviewed well and seemed to have the necessary skills to work on the projects that he would be assigned. He has been doing very good work since being hired and his manager is able to delegate many of her current assignments to him. She involves Barkley in some important decisions that she has to make for the department and has him make presentations to upper management on topics that he is more skilled in than she is. His manager is relying on him more and more to complete his projects without direct assistance from her, especially since she is often out of the office on extended business trips.

Managerial Action A

You are probably thinking that this manager has it made. She can just sit back and have Barkley do many kinds of work. That is not the case. Barkley still needs several things from his manager. He needs to be kept motivated and supported, so he will succeed at stage 4 and not slip back to a lower stage but eventually move on to stage 5. He needs to have a development plan so he can keep improving and learning and stay interested in his job. He needs to understand the culture of the department and the organization. At this productivity stage the manager manages and leads; she is "doing nothing." She can count on Barkley for the "doing."

Illustration B: The Soon-to-Be Investment Counselor

Katrina wants to succeed at her new job as an investment counselor. She is halfway through the 90-day training program and is gradually developing the skills needed to begin working with clients who are assigned to her. She can do many things on her own but needs help with others and is highly motivated to succeed.

Managerial Action B

Katrina needs to get support, be provided with practice opportunities, and receive lots of feedback—both positive and constructive. If this happens, and she has the ability, she will get to productivity stage 5.

Stage 5: Doing

In this final stage of productivity, the team member is producing at a very high level and is fully capable of doing. He may even know more than the manager. There should be no apprehension whatsoever for the manager to adopt a "do nothing" approach.

Behaviors/Actions

- ✔ Produces extremely high-quality work
- ✔ Receives the highest ratings possible on performance appraisals
- ✔ Is well respected by all those he encounters
- ✔ Often completes assignments ahead of due dates
- ✔ Can be relied on to make decisions on his own that impact his work
- ✔ Makes valuable suggestions to improve the product or service that he is engaged in

- ✔ "Walks on water"
- ✔ Can disagree strongly, but constructively, if he feels his point of view is valid
- ✔ Wants and often requests new learning experiences, new assignments, and additional opportunities for visibility
- ✔ Needs autonomy and the freedom to work on his own
- ✔ Can be a great team player when it is necessary
- ✔ Has a strong interest in advancing within the organization
- ✔ Is a risk taker and readily open to change

Illustration A: Working Her Way Up

Karen has been working for one of the largest motion picture studios for the last eighteen months, ever since graduating from college. She has gradually been working her way up within the organizational development department. She is currently responsible for executive education. She reports directly to the manager of strategic planning, who is new to his position. Karen thinks she is ready to take on that job but is willing to wait a bit longer for a promotion. She loves her job, works very hard, and receives excellent feedback from everyone. Being involved in executive development, she has met most of the senior staff and senses she made a very good impression on them. She is willing to take on any assignment or project given her and will guarantee that it is done to perfection. She prides herself on having the ability to pick up new skills on her own very quickly.

Managerial Action A

When managing a stage 5 team member, managers are able to "do nothing." Remember doing nothing means that you have the team member doing while you are managing and leading. Here, it is practically all leading. Managing takes a backseat because the team member can plan, organize, execute, and monitor her work on her own and get outstanding results. Leading behavior becomes essential with any team member at productivity stage 5. The manager needs to find chances for growth and visibility and to keep the person functioning at this high level of productivity. Positive feedback is imperative, as is finding more tangible ways to reward the individual, possibly with bonuses, incentive programs, and opportunities for promotion. It is important to note that you cannot hold on to stage 5 employees forever. Part of leading them is letting them advance as far as they can in your unit or department and, if necessary, encouraging them to move on. In fact, the best managers I have ever known or worked for recognized this need in their stage 5 team members and made sure they tried to find them new avenues to succeed in, whether within or outside of the organization.

Illustration B: The Super-Dedicated

Davis is a designer with a beverage-bottling company. He is part of the design, research, and marketing department. Davis's specific job is to design labels for water bottles and to test-market them for consumer reaction. Davis loves his job. He comes in before anyone else and is often the last one to leave. He consistently has received glowing performance appraisals. He is totally driven by what he does. His goal is to produce the best label design of any water-bottling company and to have each and every customer passionate about the labels. At the company's last holiday party, he surveyed over fifty guests (employees and their family members, including their children, and customers) on what they look for in water bottle labels. At meetings he can talk for hours, if permitted to do so, about his designs and the feedback he gets from consumers. He strongly disagrees with anyone who has a differing opinion. He can present an endless array of research findings to back up his points.

Managerial Action B

It sounds as if Davis has carried things a bit too far. Productivity stage 5 team members often become totally consumed by their jobs. They come to think of the services or products that they are part of as their own. That's great. But when they believe they know more than anyone else, or that their opinion can be the *only* opinion, or that their job is the only job that matters, then they lose perspective on the bigger picture and the manager needs to step in. The manager needs to give these team members some feedback on their behavior because they may not even realize what they are doing.

Training and Delegating: The Two Supportive Skills of Developing Others

Training

Training is the process of teaching others new skills and behaviors in order to develop them for their current or future jobs. One of the biggest responsibilities a manager has is to train the staff. Once the staff members have the requisite skills and/or behaviors necessary to perform their jobs at high-productivity stages, the manager can do nothing while they do the doing. There are ten essential ingredients for successfully training others. Keep these in mind when training or teaching others to train.

Training Essentials

1. Follow these six steps to ensure that individuals will develop by "gaining control" of their jobs:

   Step A. Define and describe or demonstrate how to do the task or job.

   Step B. Describe the importance or impact of the job and how it helps the unit, department, or organization meet its goals.

   Step C. Ascertain how much the individual being trained already knows about how to perform the job or task.

   Step D. Fill in the gaps or provide necessary training.

Step E. Allow employees to demonstrate that they have learned the skill or behavior.

Step F. Offer feedback—positive feedback—if they have done well, or constructive feedback, if they need additional help.

2. Give employees the time and resources to perform the job well.

3. Describe the standards of performance for each job or task. Trainees who know precisely what is expected of them are much more apt to invest energy in achieving their goals, and they'll probably get there faster.

4. Actively engage employees in the training. Let them ask questions, experiment, make mistakes, and offer their suggestions or opinions.

5. Give employees a chance to apply what they have just learned, the sooner the better. Adults forget 50 percent of what they have learned within one week if they do not apply it.

6. Let employees evaluate their own work, without having to rely on the trainer, once the training is complete and employees are performing the new task or skill.

7. Make sure that the skill or behavior being taught is one that the department or organization needs and is considered valuable and useful.

8. Try to incorporate all methods of learning in your training. Many managers have a method of training that they feel most comfortable with. For example, some like to use PowerPoint presentations while others would rather engage the employee through discussion or demonstration. Employees learn differently. Some learn best visually, others respond to auditory techniques, and still others learn hands-on experience.

9. Make sure everyone you intend to train needs the training. Some employees already know how to do a task but do not perform it on the job. They do not need training! Instead, find out why they aren't applying their skill on the job and rectify those issues. Robert F. Mager, a renowned expert on

training and development, said that managers have to distinguish between "can't do" (i.e., because you don't have the skills) and "won't do" (i.e., you have the skills but for some reason are not applying them). It is not a "can't do" if the team member has performed a task in the past or has done something very similar to what the manager is asking him to do now.

10. Find the right person to do the training. Although you, as the manager, are responsible for training the staff, you may not be the best suited for the job. You may not be knowledgeable enough, or you may not feel comfortable training others. In these cases, it is imperative to find someone else on staff or from outside the organization who can do the training. Don't feel bad if this occurs. Remember, a manager doesn't have to know—and cannot be expected to know—how to do everything!

Delegating

Delegating is the process of communicating to others how to perform work that the manager is currently doing. The purpose is to develop the people on the staff so they can reach higher stages of productivity so the manager can do less doing and more managing and leading. The best way for employees to develop their skills and abilities is to work on challenging assignments that push them to go beyond their current productivity stage.

Delegation focuses on how to develop employees' competencies and abilities by providing them opportunities to take on more responsibilities. Delegating is not "doling out" work. Doling out is work that has to get done but doesn't necessarily develop the person doing the work. Doling out is often the reality of managing. Do not confuse it, however, with delegation. Following are the four most important guidelines for effective delegation.

Effective Delegation

1. *Assume responsibility for the completion of any assignment or task, even with productivity stage 5 employees.* Delegation does not mean abdication of work responsibility. Even

though you, as manager, have someone else "doing" some of your job, you still need to make sure it is being done correctly and on time. You don't want to be surprised at the end that the work was not done the way you thought it would.

2. *Hold the team member accountable for completing the assignment on time and up to the standards set.* Although you have the ultimate responsibility for the assignment and cannot blame others if the assignment does not go well, you can still hold team members accountable for the results.

3. *Make sure that authority has been transferred to those who are delegated to.* Often the individuals you delegate work to will need the cooperation and assistance and support of others to succeed. They also have to get the resources that they need.

4. *Effectively communicate what you are delegating.* This is crucial. By now, accidental managers should realize that they need to delegate to develop others, and they need to find the best person for the delegation of work. But what they often forget to do is clearly communicate what the assignment is and the expectations involved. They blame the individual to whom they delegate when things get messed up. The manager needs to take the blame here. If you want to make sure you are effectively communicating a delegation, follow these steps:

   ✔ Before meeting with the team member, make sure you clearly understand what you are delegating, why you have chosen this individual, and exactly what you need to communicate to the team member.

   ✔ When meeting with the team member, first give an overview of what the project, task, or assignment is.

   ✔ Explain to the team member why you have selected him, the importance of the work, how it fits into the department's goals, and the benefits to the team member. Those benefits can include increased responsibility, skill development, improved marketability, more visibility, and more interesting work.

   ✔ Get the team member's commitment. Whenever team members agree to do something they take ownership. They are more likely to succeed if you have gotten them to buy into the task. If, however, they don't want to take on this job, you then have two choices: You can delegate the job to someone else or treat it as a doling out. A doling out is getting team members to do work that just has to be done. In this case, managers should make it clear that the work being assigned isn't a delegation or a growth opportunity.

✔ Describe in detail the assignment. What will the team member have to do? What are the recommended procedures, time frames, etc.? Provide training if necessary. Encourage the team member to ask questions and offer suggestions. She may have a better or just a different way of doing something. Management guru Peter Drucker said that the people closest to the service or product probably know best, so why not ask them. Sometimes, you may not want to give the team member all of the details on a particular assignment. You may want to challenge your team members as a way of developing them and have them figure out what needs to be done on their own. With productivity stage 4 and 5 staff members, you may have even less explaining to do.

✔ Set up periodic reviews to guarantee that your team members grasp the assignment and are carrying out their new responsibility. The amount of monitoring that you need to do will depend on the complexity of the responsibility and the productivity stage of the team member.

✔ Give feedback throughout the delegation process. Give positive feedback when team members are performing well or are improving and constructive feedback if you need to "realign" them.

✔ Be available, to as great an extent as possible, whenever a team member has a need.

Chapter Summary

Platinum skills are the crucial skills needed by successful managers. Developing others is the first of these skills. Developing staff members involves recognizing the five productivity stages of development—attention getting, flying blind, steadiness, on the rise, and doing—and then determining what managerial actions to take at each of these stages. This chapter gave strategies for how to implement the two supportive skills of developing others: training and delegating. Once managers have begun to develop their teams, they will find that the use of the other Platinum skills of active listening, giving and receiving feedback, and motivating (discussed in the next three chapters) will enable their team members to get to productivity stages 4 and 5 easier and faster. A primary role—if not *the* primary role—of the manager is to develop team members. You have to train team members how to perform many new responsibilities successfully. Too often managers neglect this very important function because they don't have the time. One thing is clear: Managers can never gain time by doing the work themselves. They can only gain time by training their team members and then delegating to them. Developing others is an investment in a better future for the individual team member, the department, and the organization.

CHAPTER 5

The Platinum Skill of Active Listening

Active listening is not only listening for meaning and understanding (which is fairly easy for most people), but also listening to let the other person know that he has been listened to (which is the real challenge). We also need to be aware of our nonverbal behaviors because how we react and present ourselves influences how others listen to us. Think of some of the bad listeners you know. They probably have these habits:

- ✔ They make comments or ask questions that having nothing to do with what you have just said.
- ✔ They never look at you.
- ✔ They multitask (e.g., work on their computer or talk on their phone while they are listening to you).
- ✔ They look bored, uninterested.
- ✔ They have one expression on their face throughout the conversation.
- ✔ They fidget (e.g., play with their pencil or objects on their desk).
- ✔ They walk away as you are talking and say, "Keep going, I am listening."
- ✔ They fake attention and pretend to listen.
- ✔ They never ask questions, clarify, or paraphrase.

✔ They finish your sentences for you or interrupt when you are talking.

How do you feel when you are on the receiving end of a bad listener? Pretty bummed out, I would imagine. These are just some of the bad listening habits we want to avoid as managers. Bad listening is bad for business. We may miss information that is vital to our work; sever relationships with colleagues, bosses, and employees; never reach a clarity of understanding; and decrease the morale of those not being listened to. All of these results impact the quality of the work, which impacts productivity and profitability.

In this chapter we examine why listening is such a difficult skill. We look at the "noise" factors that prevent us from listening effectively, the different styles of listening, several types of active-listening and nonverbal-listening skills, and the influence that culture has on listening. The major purpose for being an excellent listener, as a manager, is to support the development of your team members. When your team members feel and believe that you are listening to what they say, it greatly helps them become "on the rise" and "doing" team members performing at productivity stages 4 and 5, respectively. They are able to do more of the "doing" so the manager can do more managing and leading.

Why Listening Is So Difficult

Listening is one of the most difficult skills. Very few people have ever had training in how to listen. It is estimated that most of us only listen at about 30 percent of our capacity. That means we are missing 70 percent of the message, or 70 percent of all the messages sent to us. Listening is such a difficult skill to acquire mainly because of three factors:

1. *Committee of People*. I know you are earnestly reading this book right now and concentrating on the information being given to you. But I would bet at this moment you are thinking about many other things as well. You may be thinking about what you'll have for lunch or dinner, how your afternoon meeting will go, who's picking up the kids today, or

you're thinking about whether he or she will call later, sex, or your recent or upcoming vacation. This is normal behavior, and our psychologist friends tell us it is very healthy as well. What is happening is that there's a committee of people (not real people, of course) traveling with us wherever we go that's always trying to take us away from the situation. Our committee of people is particularly with us when we are bored or uninterested in the situation or conversation at hand. But the committee is also with us at the most opportune or important listening times in our lives.

For example, years ago I was listening to a television news program where Barbara Walters was interviewing former presidents. She was asking them all different types of questions. One of the questions was, "When you were taking the oath of office for the president of the United States, what were you thinking at that time?" Now, on one hand, I cannot believe what these presidents admitted to. On the other hand, I realize it takes great self-assuredness to admit your thoughts. I remember one of the responses quite well. President Carter said that the day he was elected president his wife gave him a new attaché case with his initials on it. When he was taking the oath of office a few months later and listening to the Chief Supreme Court Justice, he was trying to remember where he had put the attaché case, because he wanted to take it to the Oval Office on his first day of work. This story illustrates the reality of, and the power of, the committee of people. Some of the other presidents spoke of even more minor things. So when you are talking to your team members and they are telling you about a new business opportunity or a major glitch in the computer system, be careful; your committee of people may have taken you away.

2. *Human Brain Physiology*. The human brain is too developed or sophisticated for the listening process. It can do so many other things at the same time. This is another reason why listening is so difficult. Unless we have been trained, or have practiced a lot, it is difficult for most of us to focus on one person or one conversation at a time.

3. *Noise Factors*. Noise factors are barriers to listening. They are the specific things that prevent us from listening to oth-

ers. Noise factors can be either internally (our own personal barriers) or externally (from the other person or the environment) generated. There are literally hundreds, maybe thousands, of these noise factors. Here's just a partial listing of these noise factors:

Internal Noise Factors

✔ Your emotional state (e.g., angry, anxious, depressed, stressed)

✔ Your physiological state (e.g., hard of hearing, poor eyesight)

✔ Illness or well-being (e.g., backache, the flu, overly tired)

✔ Personal biases, prejudices, perceptions, assumptions

✔ Thinking about what you will say instead of listening to the speaker

✔ Preoccupation with your own issues or situation, having your own agenda

✔ Mind reading what the other person is thinking or feeling

✔ Searching for the right kind of advice or recommendations to give

✔ Going to any lengths to avoid being wrong

✔ Placating because you want people to like you

✔ Personal values and beliefs

External Noise Factors

✔ Language differences

✔ Difficulty understanding accents or word pronunciations

✔ Speaker's use of slang or jargon or acronyms that you are not familiar with

✔ A boring subject or topic, or a topic you have heard a hundred times before

✔ Monotonous or monotone voice of the speaker

✔ The workplace environment (e.g., room temperature too hot or too cold)

    ✔ Background noise (e.g., machines running, pagers going off, phones ringing, alarms, or sirens that impede your ability to hear)

    ✔ The personality, grooming, appearance, or attire of the speaker

    ✔ The speaker's title or position within the organization

Let me share a few real examples from employees as to how these noise factors can be barriers to listening effectively.

Example 1: Multiple Meanings

Fiona works in a department store in Boston. Recently she was in her boss's office discussing the store's merchandise return policy. In the middle of the meeting, the boss received a phone call. She told Fiona to come back in a short time and they would resume the meeting. Fiona did as she was told. She came back in twenty minutes. The boss was furious when Fiona walked into her office. She said, "I told you to come back in a short time. Where were you?" Fiona said, "I gave you a short time to finish your call, twenty minutes." The boss yelled, "You don't know what the word short means. It means five minutes!" Because both Fiona and her boss had different meanings for the word *short*, it caused their communication problem. The noise factor at hand was vocabulary. One word can be a noise factor. The unclear meaning of this word affected the listening process between Fiona and her boss. In order to have avoided this barrier, the boss could have been more specific about the time frame or could have arranged to notify Fiona when she was finished with her call. Fiona could have been an active listener and asked what her boss meant by "a short time," or she could have come back periodically to see if the boss was ready.

Have you ever received an e-mail that read, "I need this ASAP?" What does ASAP (as soon as possible) mean to you? Do you drop whatever you are doing or get it to the person by the end of the day, or the end of the week? As managers, we need to be very careful about the words we use and make sure we are being clear, concise, and precise when we are communicating. Often our team members are embarrassed to speak up or ask for clarification when they do not understand something or are confused. It is our responsibility to encourage them to do so. In fact, if you want to prove this point about the perils of not speaking up and have a little fun at your next meeting, make up an acronym, say PACS, and use it in the explanation of something. What do you think will happen? Most likely nobody will respond or question you about the meaning of the acronym. In today's work environment, no one wants to appear that they are ignorant or not familiar with the latest company buzzword.

Example 2: Values

Values are our strongly held feelings and thoughts about right or wrong. We believe that our values are the right ones to have, when in reality, they are just our values.

Jennifer, a new sales manager at a hard-disk manufacturing company, had a difficult decision to make. She had to select one of her four sales associates to go overseas for a two-month business trip. All four of her staff members were at productivity stage 4, so it was an especially tough decision. Jennifer almost immediately eliminated Jon. At the outset of their conversation about the upcoming assignment, he mentioned that he and his wife had planned for the possibility of his traveling for the job and they would make alternative arrangements for child care since Jon's wife worked evenings. Jennifer believed that someone with young children cannot and should not be away from home for long periods of time. Jennifer immediately stopped listening to Jon during the meeting. She never heard that Jon had experience working in that region of the world and that he also spoke the language. Jennifer's values on family life and business travel became a barrier to her effective listening. It is possible that Jon was the best candidate for this assignment. If she was wrong, Jennifer's decision may hurt Jon's career. He may be viewed as someone who does not travel for the organization, and Jennifer, because of her strongly held values, may have eliminated him from other projects that involve travel or working late.

Managers are often unaware of how their values impact their managing. The manager's values and beliefs influence what projects team members are assigned to, what clients they get to meet, which presentations they are allowed to make, how their performance is appraised, their promotional opportunities, and anything else that might influence their success within the organization. The manager's values ultimately affect the success of the organization.

Example 3: Personality

Patrick works for a Management Knocker (one of the types of "worst" managers from Chapter 2). The Management Knocker continually complains about the job of managing and the upper management of the organization. For months now that is all Patrick hears when he has his monthly meeting with his boss. The meeting is intended to make sure projects are on track. But his work progress and whether he is meeting his goals is a small part of the meeting. Once the boss begins to complain, Patrick finds it very difficult, if not impossible, to actively listen to her. He finds her personality to be annoying and negative. When she does mention something more relevant to him about one of his projects, he often does not hear her because he has stopped listening. Patrick has allowed his committee of people to take him away from the situation.

These three examples demonstrate the power of noise factors or barriers and how they can influence the listening situation. As managers, we need to recognize which internal noise factors we are guilty of and what we can do about them and what we can do to reduce any external noise factors. The more we can reduce the impact of these barriers, the more motivating the listening experiences of our team members will be. The more motivating these experiences are for them, the easier it will be for them to advance to or remain at the higher productivity stages.

Because of noise factors, human brain physiology, and the committee of people, listening is a difficult skill to master. Being aware of the challenges to effective listening is the first step toward becoming an active listener. But being able to use the right listening style at the right time, using nonverbal-listening strategies, and being aware of cultural differences in communicating will also enable managers to be effective listeners.

Different Styles of Listening

The five styles of listening are:

1. Comprehensive
2. Fact-Finding
3. Directive
4. Empathetic
5. Appreciative

It is important that managers are able to use *all of the styles* in developing their team members. The style used should depend on the listening situation the manager is in. Different styles are required for different situations. For example, if a manager needs to calm down a team member and reassure him, then the manager would use the empathetic style.

Many managers tend to overuse the listening style(s) that they feel most comfortable with or have had the most practice with. They are often unaware that they do not use a certain style at all. Other managers feel comfortable with all styles, but they use them at the wrong time! For example, when they should be listening in a directive mode, they are being empathetic, or when they should be listening comprehensively, they are being appreciative. Let's take a closer look at these five listening styles.

Comprehensive

Managers who prefer or use this style listen for the entire message. They try to comprehend everything that is being communicated to them. The comprehensive style of listening works best for those situations where a lot of information is being shared and where the manager needs to get an overview or overall summary of what has been said to her. For example, a manager's employees might be giving her all the reasons why they feel their team is not working effectively together and what they believe can be done to remedy the situation. Knowing all of the facts and information will help the manager make a decision about what to do. To be a comprehensive listener you have to be patient, allow the other person(s) to talk, ask open-ended questions, clarify your understanding throughout (which will be discussed later in this chapter), and summarize what you have heard.

Open-ended questions require longer, more complex answers and draw out a wide range of responses. Examples of open-ended questions include:

- ✔ What are a few examples of how the team is not working together?

- ✔ What are several additional strategies for building team spirit?

- ✔ Think of the best teams you have ever been on. What made those teams work so well together?

- ✔ Could you elaborate on what you mean by "team barriers"?

Summarize at the end of a conversation. If it is a lengthy discussion, then summarize at intermittent points. A summary statement may be something like this:

"Let me summarize what I understood you to say. You said (a) _____, (b) _____, and (c) _____. Now, was there anything else affecting the problem?"

Managers who do not prefer the comprehensive style of listening are often time pressured or impatient; they may not value the thoughts and opinions of their staff, or are not comfortable communicating with others.

Fact-Finding

Managers who prefer this style listen only for specific information. They need to find out a date, or the third step in the new procedure, or how much the client is willing to pay. They tune out everything else and only listen for what they need to know. To be a fact-finding listener, tell your employee what information you are looking for. Then ask specific, direct, or close-ended questions. Direct questions require a short answer; close-ended questions require a yes or no response. Examples are:

- ✔ Did you reply to the customer by three o'clock today?
- ✔ Which profile form did you insert in the shipment?
- ✔ What price did we charge last year?
- ✔ When did you first discover the problem?

Managers who do not prefer this style of listening like to engage in lengthy discussions and see the big picture. They want to know everything and find it difficult to have brief listening experiences.

Directive

Some managers prefer to listen in order to direct someone to do something. Directing can also include offering advice and attempting to do the thinking for the speaker. This listening strategy may be effective with employees at the lower productivity stages. But it should be avoided as much as possible with employees at the higher stages because you want them to do the thinking. To be a directive listener you have to be able to tell someone what to do and why it needs to be done that way. Here are some examples:

Example 1

Employee: I am having problems with Andy. He never gives me the information that I need to complete the customer profile unless I ask him six or seven times.

Directive Listener (manager): Come to me the next time it happens and I will speak with Andy and get you what you need.

Example 2

Team Member: I just cannot get along with the marketing department. They never give me a straight answer.

Directive Listener (manager): Let me give you some advice. When dealing with marketing this is what you have to do. First, _____.

Managers who do not prefer to use the directive style find it difficult to tell others what to do or come across as the expert. They either want the other person to make the decision or come to a joint decision.

Empathetic

The empathetic listener allows a team member to talk without feeling that he's being criticized or judged. The empathetic listener also listens to and acknowledges the feeling and the emotions that the person is experiencing. Being an empathetic listener is appropriate when someone is going through a difficult time at work or in his personal life, has just had a setback at work, or is stressed or overburdened. A manager can also express empathy when someone is feeling happy, elated, or excited.

A large part of being an empathetic listener is to listen to nonverbal communication—that is, the other person's body language and tone of voice.

Of all of the listening styles, empathetic listener is the hardest one for most managers. It takes a lot of practice and willingness to recognize the feelings and emotions of others and to be supportive of how they are feeling. The idea is not to say that they are right or wrong for feeling that way, but just to recognize what they are going through. Feelings are not right or wrong. They just are. When someone's feelings or emotions are acknowledged, that person knows the manager is really listening.

Example 1

Team Member: I completed the project early and the client just sent me this congratulatory note. Take a look at it!

Empathetic Listener (manager): You sound so proud and happy. That's great.

Example 2

Team Member: I am having such a tough time with our new client. She immediately agrees and then days later changes her mind.

Empathetic Listener (manager): You sound very distressed and frustrated. Dealing with clients is one of the most challenging things. I have had some very difficult ones as well. I know what you are going through.

Managers who do not use the empathetic style find it hard to recognize and acknowledge their own feelings and emotions and the feelings and emotions of others. They also believe that feelings should not be part of the workplace. These managers may not think it is appropriate to disclose anything about their personal lives, either.

Appreciative

At times we need to listen to a team member in an appreciative way. She may be telling you about one of her great accomplishments or have a very interesting "war story" for you. She may be telling you how great her daughter did in last Saturday's soccer game. As an appreciative listener, you just listen. You do not ask questions or add your opinion. You acknowledge what they are saying, verbally or nonverbally.

Of all the listening styles, this one is used the least. Time pressures and the increasing focus on task and the bottom line in most organizations has caused this style of listening to decrease. But those managers who can listen in an appreciative way build rapport, trust, and a constructive working relationship with their team.

Example

Team Member: Last week I finally got to meet Mr. G and, boy, was I nervous, after all the terrible things I had heard about him. But I figured out how to handle him.

Appreciative Listener (manager): Tell me.

Team Member: Well, early on, I realized that if I was going to get him on my side, I would have to let him do all the talking. And did it work! Let me tell you how I figured this out.

Appreciative Listener: I can't wait to hear. (leans in close and lowers voice)

Appreciative listening is difficult for managers who are only task focused. If a team member is not communicating something vital or informative, they will stop listening. They just do not see the value in it.

Once again, managers need to be aware of which styles they are not comfortable with and practice them more. They also need to be aware if they are misusing any of these styles. That is, are they using the wrong style for the particular listening situation? Mismatches between what the situation calls for and the listening style used may lead team members to believe that they are not being listened to.

Active-Listening Skills

Active listening means *demonstrating* to the speaker that the speaker has been heard. Active listening also means *creating a shared meaning* between listener and speaker. Managers demonstrate and create shared meaning by using verbal and nonverbal-listening responses. The listening responses include clarifying, acknowledging, self-disclosure, and maintaining congruence. These four skills will be discussed at length later in this chapter, along with the nonverbal-listening responses and the relationship between culture and listening. First, though, I want to share some overall listening habits of the most effective listeners. I call these the eleven habits of highly effective listeners.

The Eleven Habits of Highly Effective Listeners

1. *Highly effective listeners work at listening.* They realize listening is composed of many skills and that it takes practice to improve these skills. They practice their listening skills every opportunity they have.

2. *Highly effective listeners look for a common area of interest in the speaker's message.* They view listening as an oppor-

tunity to find out information or to learn more about the speaker.

3. *Highly effective listeners maintain an open mind.* Even if they disagree with what the speaker has to say, they do not shut down. They still listen to understand the other person's point of view without getting judgmental. They also watch out for triggers (words, expressions, or actions from the speaker) that would immediately put them in an emotional state. They try to remain calm and constructive.

4. *Highly effective listeners avoid distractions.* They understand that anything can be a distraction to a speaker. They try to limit distractions such as the phone or pager going off, working on other things while they are listening, and playing with objects on their desks. They give their full attention to the speaker.

5. *Highly effective listeners ask for feedback.* They ask others for constructive feedback on how they come across in listening situations. When appropriate, they use videotaping as another way of getting feedback.

6. *Highly effective listeners can separate content from delivery.* A big part of listening is to listen to everything the speaker presents, not just her words. However, it is also imperative to focus on the message and separate it from the speaker's appearance, dress, accent, and job title.

7. *Highly effective listeners comprehend nonverbal communication.* They are able to pick up meaning not only through the speaker's words but also through his voice inflection or tone, rapidity of speech, facial expression, body movement, and hand gestures.

8. *Highly effective listeners use active listening to help them make decisions.* They listen to others' points of view, opinions, knowledge, and experience. This enables them to make sounder decisions.

9. *Highly effective listeners know that hearing and listening are very different.* Anyone lucky enough to have the physiological capability can hear sounds and words. Your most effective listeners use active listening. They interpret the words and nonverbal behaviors, derive meaning from them, and let the speaker know that he or she was understood.

10. *Highly effective listeners always have a goal in mind when they are listening.* They try to accomplish something during each of their listening encounters. The goal may be fact-finding or comprehension or directive, or to be an apprecia- tive listener or empathetic one.

11. *Highly effective listeners know that pretending to listen is not better than admitting that they are not interested or do not have the time to listen.* Your best listeners will let others know if they are not prepared to listen at that moment and, if possible, they try to set up another time when they will be able to give 100 percent of their attention to the speaker. They may have deadlines to meet, or they may be under a lot of stress or right in the middle of an important project. I have met many ingenious managers over the years who found ways to "subtly" hint that they do not have the time to listen. Let me share several examples:

   ✔ A manager in the travel-related division of American Express puts police tape in her office doorway when she is working on an important assignment and doesn't have the time to listen.

   ✔ A manager at Microsoft always stands up when someone enters his cubicle. This immediately sends the message to oth- ers that the manager doesn't have the time to listen now.

   ✔ Many managers set time limits. They say that they have ten minutes to spare, and if that isn't enough time, then they sug- gest meeting later.

   ✔ A manager at Disney Imaginary says he is working on a special project for Michael Eisner (Disney's CEO). It always works. People leave his office immediately.

   ✔ Some managers angle their desks and chairs so they aren't facing the opening to their office or cubicle. Many studies have shown that when managers and their desks face the entranceway to their office, they get many more visitors. The trick is to angle the desk about forty-five degrees so that when someone passes an open door or space and looks in (they may have passed it a thousand times but they will still look in) eye contact isn't made. Eye contact encourages or obliges some- one to speak.

Effective listeners try not to pretend to listen because, eventually, the speaker will know that they are not being active listeners. Obviously, there are times and situations when we may have to pretend to listen because we don't want to hurt someone's feelings or tell the person we are not interested or do not have the time. At one time or another, even the best listeners have pretended to listen to the boss, the customer, and the mother-in-law. Psychologists tell us that we should never pretend to listen to our children. These are the listening situations that really challenge us. The best listeners use all of their listening skills in these situations and before long, they are not pretending, they are actively listening.

Clarifying, Acknowledging, Self-Disclosure, and Maintaining Congruence

Figure 5-1 lists the four types of active-listening responses, examples of which follow.

Figure 5-1. The active-listening skills.

Clarifying. To clarify means to state in your own words what you believe the team member has said. Clarifying can also mean asking questions to make sure you have understood the message or to find out additional information that will help you understand the message. Your most effective listeners clarify throughout a conversation. Even if they understand exactly what the team member has said they would still want to occasionally clarify to let the team member know that they are actively listening. Clarifying has big benefits for the manager and the team member:

- ✔ Team members appreciate being heard and understood. It lets them know that their manager is interested in what they are saying.

- ✔ Clarifying helps the manager remember what he has heard.

- ✔ Clarifying prevents misunderstandings and inaccurate assumptions.

- ✔ The manager stays better focused by asking for clarification instead of allowing noise factors or the committee of people from preventing understanding.

- ✔ If the team member is in an emotional state (e.g., angry), clarifying can reduce the strength of the emotional reaction and get the conversation back on track.

- ✔ Clarifying saves the manager time and money. By checking for understanding, he avoids future problems that can take valuable time to correct or can be financially costly. Clarifying makes good business sense.

Here are three sample conversations where the manager is using the active-listening technique of clarification (the clarifying comments are in italics):

Example 1

Employee: Our current procedural steps seem to be outdated. We could get the deliveries out to the customers in half the time it currently takes if we followed different procedures.

Manager (the clarifier): *It is your opinion that we need to take a look at our current procedures for customer delivery.*

Example 2

Team Member: I hear there's a new software package that will save us a lot of time in tracking our shipments. My friend over at SJ Industries uses it and they have reduced tracking time by 80 percent.

Manager: *That's great. We need to look into something like that. It would save us a lot of time and trouble.*

Example 3

Team Member: I explained to the team what the new docking procedures were and gave them a few examples of what I meant. But when I went to check their forms, it was as if I never explained anything to them.

Manager: *Did you check their understanding of the new procedures before you let them fill out the forms?*

Acknowledging. When we acknowledge we let the speaker know that we are still engaged in the conversation and that our committee of people has not taken us elsewhere. We acknowledge when we want and need to prolong the conversation and/or keep it flowing. Acknowledging encourages the speaker to continue. Once again, we are not giving our opinions or disagreeing with the speaker. We just want to hear what the other person is saying. We can acknowledge by using very short verbal statements such as: "I hear you," "I see," "Keep going," "I'm following you," "Okay," "Right," "Oh," "Interesting," and "Uh-huh." We can also acknowledge nonverbally using facial expressions, body language, or hand gestures. Examples include:

- ✔ Raising an eyebrow (suggests you aren't sure or are unclear and you need the other person to tell you more)
- ✔ Smiling (shows you are in agreement)

✔ Leaning a bit closer (demonstrates that you are very interested in what the person is saying)

✔ Nodding your head (shows agreement)

✔ Maintaining eye contact (lets the person know you are following her)

✔ Putting your palms up, facing the speaker (gives the message to stop, telling the speaker you're not following what she is saying)

Acknowledging helps build rapport and trust. We are letting the speaker know that he has been understood. It demonstrates to the speaker that the manager has listened actively. When the manager acknowledges, he is acting as a sounding board, allowing the speaker to bounce off ideas, plans, thoughts, and feelings. When acknowledging, the manager is not being critical, judgmental, or opinionated.

Self-Disclosure. Mark Golden manages the customer services training unit in his company. He has been managing for about two years. Let's listen in on part of a discussion Mark is having with one of his staff members, Alan:

Mark: Let me share with you my thoughts and feelings on the reorganization. I believe that the proposed merger between our unit and the technical sales training unit will be very beneficial to us and to the company as well. It will give us more insight into how our systems get sold and which features of our systems the customers like. It will help us when we are training the customers. I'm really behind this merger and will do everything possible to make it work.

Alan: I agree with you, and I understand the benefits, but I'm sure some of us will lose our jobs as a result.

Mark: I know that's always a concern. I have that concern and I am feeling scared as well. I enjoy managing this unit and I would hate to have to give it up.

Mark is using the active-listening skill of self-disclosure. He is communicating information about how he feels and what he is thinking. These are his true feeling and thoughts. When managers self-disclose they do not distort, lie, or have masks on. They share with others the truth. Self-disclosure builds trust and closeness between the manager and his employees. When Mark used self-disclosure, it opened the door for Alan to do the same. Self-disclosure encourages self-disclosure. Self-disclosure can also refer to sharing factual knowledge about what's going on in the business unit, department, or organization. Self-disclosure leads to better working relationships and improved communication.

Too much self-disclosure can be just as detrimental as not enough. Managers who constantly share every thought, feeling, and bit of information with their staff are overdoing it.

Maintaining Congruence. Ira Kelm has been managing for a few months and recently took over a group that was previously managed by someone else. He finds it very hard to listen to his group because of his time pressures. He is working on so many assignments that he doesn't have time to breathe, much less handle new managerial and administrative responsibilities as well. His group comprises recent college graduates. They are very smart, but they don't know what they are doing. They have all of these questions that Ira cannot believe they ask. The answers seem so obvious to him. He has to grin and bear it, though. He is trying to be supportive and help them out and feels he listens to them quite effectively. Last week he had a department meeting and asked his group of five employees to give him feedback on how they thought he was doing as their new manager. They were a bit hesitant to do so, but with some coaxing from Ira, they acquiesced. They gave him high marks on his technical abilities and his knowledge of the business environment. However, they said he was a terrible listener. They acknowledged that he would spend time with them and gave them good advice, but they always got the sense he would rather be doing something else. They attributed this to his nonverbal behavior. For example, they said he rolled his eyes a lot, didn't maintain eye contact, worked on something else at the same time he was listening, sighed often, and frowned when he was telling them something positive or trying to encourage them. His verbal behavior, his words, were not in sync with his nonverbal behavior. They were getting a mixed message.

The group was not getting *congruence*. Ira was communicating one message with his words (knowledge, support) and another message with his nonverbal behavior (disinterest, boredom). When we are communicating or listening our message must be congruent. There has to be a match between verbal and nonverbal behavior.

Listening Nonverbally

One of my first jobs was working for a major medical center in New York State. I was part of the organizational development (OD) department, which was headed by one of those worst types of managers. Glenn Stark was the unpredictable type. One day he would be your best friend, friendly, communicative, and approachable. The next day he would be a tyrant. He would yell, ridicule, and be dictatorial. However, being able to read or "listen" to Glenn's nonverbal behaviors proved to be helpful to my success and the success of my colleagues in the OD department. I will never forget what I am about to describe, and this occurred over twenty years ago. Every morning I would gather my colleagues and we would go to the window in our offices that faced the parking lot. We would watch the way Glenn pulled into his parking spot and how he would get out of his car and walk into the building. If he slammed the car door, had a "mean" look on his face, walked very rapidly, or was pounding his fist into the newspaper we knew to keep away from Glenn. He was in a bad mood, and if we went anywhere near him, life would be miserable for us. On the other hand, if he had a smile on his face, waved to other people, held the building door open for others, or had an uplifting gait, we would approach him and get whatever we wanted!

As we have already discussed, we listen in two major ways: verbally and nonverbally. Most communication experts believe that about 75 percent of meaning is derived from nonverbal communication and only about 25 percent from verbal. Being able to listen nonverbally to others at work is essential for managerial success. Also, keep in mind that as a manager, your employees are continually interpreting your nonverbal communication.

Nonverbal-listening responses fall into several categories: vocal, body language, facial expressions/eye contact, and proximity. Here are some suggestions for increasing effectiveness in each of the categories.

Vocal

When we listen vocally or when others are listening to us vocally, meaning is acquired through voice tone, rate/pace of speech, volume, and pronunciation/articulation.

- ✔ *Tone* refers to the quality and pitch of the voice. A manager needs to speak with a well-modulated tone, varying emphasis depending on what is being said. Managers need to avoid the one-pitch tone. A monotonous voice is a noise factor and makes the listening experience very boring.

- ✔ *Rate/pace* refers to how fast or slow you speak. Managers who speak too fast or slow or who never vary the pace lose the listener.

- ✔ *Volume* refers to how loudly or softly you speak. Many listeners find a voice that is too loud to be aggressive behavior. They feel the speaker is trying to get his way at the expense of the listener. When the speaker's voice is too low, the listener feels as if the speaker doesn't want to self-disclose or isn't interested in communicating. The listener also misses what could be important information.

- ✔ *Pronunciation/articulation* refers to how you say your words—your accent, diction, and inflection. In today's multinational and multicultural workplaces, we must be aware that even though most people speak English, words are often pronounced differently. In addition, understanding different accents can be difficult. As a manager, you may feel that you are articulating your words correctly. You may be. That is no guarantee, however, that all of your employees will understand you. You may think you do not have an accent, but to someone from a different country or even a different region in the United States, you have an accent. Managers need to ask for clarification to make sure that they have been understood.

The Case of the Low Talker

Many years ago I hired Alec to assist me on some projects I was working on. He had a very soft voice and I had to ask Alec to repeat himself many times before I was able to hear him. I gave him feedback on his vocal quality, but he never changed. His work was great, so I didn't mind that much. One day we were at lunch and I was preoccupied with some personal issues. Alec was talking to me, but I couldn't hear him. I just pretended to listen (something effective listeners shouldn't do) and I agreed to whatever he said by nodding my head or saying, "Sure, I understand." Two weeks later, on payday, Alec asked me what happened to his 20 percent raise. This time he spoke loudly. "What pay raise?" I asked. "The one you agreed to two weeks ago at lunch," he replied.

The Garage Case

Last summer I was doing a presentation in South Africa and asked a fellow speaker who I had just met to join me for a drink. During our discussion, he mentioned that as a side business he was opening a "GAR-age." I had no idea what he meant. I sat there bewildered until I finally asked him what a "GAR-age" was. You see, South Africans put the emphasis on the first syllable and Americans put it on the second (ga-RAGE—or a "garage" to you and me).

Body Language

We send messages by the way we stand, move, or sit, and what we do with our arms, legs, and head. For example, someone who stands tall and erect with a relaxed posture communicates a strong presence, self-assuredness, and assertive behavior. Someone who is hunched over, has bent knees, and fidgets a lot is communicating the opposite message. Often body language has a generally agreed-on interpretation by people with similar cultural backgrounds. For example, in some cultures having arms folded over the chest is viewed as a defensive posture, signifying someone who's not being open. It could have other meanings, however—the person could be cold or have an itch.

Body Language Suggestions

- ✔ Face the person.
- ✔ Lean slightly toward the person you are speaking with.
- ✔ Hold your head up.
- ✔ Relax your hands and arms.
- ✔ Use natural but energetic and purposeful movements.

Facial Expressions/Eye Contact

Facial expression and eye contact are the most revealing ways that demonstrate to others whether we are listening to them. By facial expressions I mean looking concerned, angry, scared, happy, annoyed, devastated, elated, etc. Other examples of facial expression include raising or lowering your eyebrows, wrinkling your forehead, and dropping your chin. A smile is also considered a facial expression. It usually signifies that the listener is being receptive to what the speaker is saying. There has been some interesting research done on smiling. Some people rarely smile, like the Task Monger manager from Chapter 2. They don't smile because it physically hurts them to do so. They aren't accustomed to using their "smile" muscles. (Some babies born without these smile muscles even require surgery.) Many managers are uncomfortable maintaining eye contact with their employees. This could be because of cultural upbringing or lack of experience in speaking directly to other people. If this is the case, they may look at the bridge of the nose, the eyebrows, or the forehead of the speaker.

Facial Expression/Eye Contact Suggestions

- ✔ Your facial expressions need to be consistent (congruent) with the feelings you are expressing.

✔ Eye contact should be direct, relaxed, and steady (not staring).

✔ You should maintain eye contact about 80 percent of the time, occasionally and briefly glancing away.

✔ If you intend to take notes during a conversation, it is always best to let the other person know or else they may think you are working on your shopping list. When taking notes, you still need to maintain eye contact at least 60–70 percent of the time.

Proximity

The physical distance or space between two people has a large impact on how successful the listening experience will be. If you are too far away, the listener will get the impression that you are not interested and really don't want to be involved in the listening situation. If you are standing too close, you have "invaded" someone's space and as soon as you do, the listening stops.

Much that is communicated in the workplace is not verbalized. As listeners and managers we need to remember that when someone is not talking, he is communicating. An important skill of successful listening is being able to listen to the vocal and visual behaviors—the nonverbals.

The Case of the Close Talker

One of the production managers I was consulting with at an aerospace company was bright, helpful, and had quite a sense of humor. But he was a "close talker." He would come right up to my face, maybe three inches away, and begin speaking. I didn't hear a word he said. He made me feel extremely uncomfortable.

Listening to Cultural Differences

People from different cultural backgrounds have learned to communicate differently. They also have different values and beliefs. As managers, we need to be aware of and be sensitive to these differences. We also need to educate ourselves about cultural differences in communication, especially nonverbal communication. The same gesture, physical movement, behavior, or facial expression may mean different things to different people. When we fail to see differences in communication or do not value or understand these differences, we have stopped listening. These three examples demonstrate the impact of cultural differences in communicating. Successful managers respect and learn what these differences are.

The Insubordinate Employee

Miguel is a supervisor in the chemistry department of a drug research firm. Weeks ago a new employee joined the department. Whenever Miguel spoke to her or asked her a question, the employee would look down and not respond. Miguel observed this behavior and assumed the employee was being rude and insubordinate. He became quite angry and annoyed with the employee. Miguel even went as far as to contact the union and bring this employee up on charges of insubordination. As it turned out, the employee was not being insubordinate. It was actually the opposite. She had learned in her country that when a boss speaks you are supposed to look down and not respond, especially if it is a male boss.

The "Okay" Gesture

In conversations in the United States we use the "okay" gesture (thumb and forefinger forming a circle) often. If, as a manager, you observed a team member using this gesture you would think everything was okay. However, in many parts of the world that gesture can be interpreted as a curse.

For the Boss

A colleague of mine who obtained a consulting job in a firm in Southeast Asia related this story to me. One day he noticed that one of the firm's staff members was very unhappy. He looked sullen and dejected. My friend went over to him and asked how everything was.

The employee said that he was distressed because of an e-mail he had received. My friend looked at the e-mail. It had thanked this staff member for doing such a great job on a particular project. My friend thought the staff member was crazy. Why would anyone get so upset about such a positive-sounding e-mail? When my friend investigated the situation, he found out that in this country's culture the boss is supposed to get all the credit, not the staff member.

Chapter Summary

Let's review the key ingredients of active listening:

1. Avoid bad listening habits, such as finishing someone else's sentence or doing another task while the other person is speaking.

2. Understand the reasons why listening is such a challenging skill. Among the reasons are noise factors, such as language or personality barriers, having your own agenda, the "committee of people" who are always trying to take you away from the current listening situation, and the fact that the brain is too developed to do just one thing at a time.

3. Learn to use all five listening styles, depending on which one is needed at the time. These listening styles are comprehensive, fact-finding, directive, empathetic, and appreciative.

4. Become comfortable with and implement the eleven habits of highly effective listeners.

5. Become good at the active-listening skills of clarifying, acknowledging, self-disclosure, and maintaining congruence.

6. Listen nonverbally by garnering meaning from the other person's voice tone, body language, facial expressions and ability to maintain eye contact, gestures, and proximity.

7. Recognize that individuals with different cultural backgrounds will communicate differently. As a manager, you need to listen to those differences.

CHAPTER 6

The Platinum Skill of Giving and Receiving Feedback

Feedback lets others know how they are doing in terms of their work-related performance and behaviors. Positive feedback tells team members exactly what they did well and why it deserves recognition. Positive feedback also encourages team members to repeat those same behaviors. Constructive feedback, often called coaching, corrects any performance or behavior issues before they become serious. This chapter discusses the five types of feedback, how to deliver both positive and constructive feedback, and how to receive feedback from team members.

The Five Types of Feedback

The five types of feedback that managers use most frequently are:

1. Negative
2. Silent or No
3. Unrelated Positive
4. Positive
5. Constructive

Negative Feedback

Not too long ago, I walked through the corridors and cubicle areas of a well-known insurance company and listened in (actually eavesdropped) on managers communicating with their staffs. These statements were just some of the ones I heard them using when they were giving feedback:

"No."

"It will never work."

"Wrong. That's not what I wanted!"

"Those aren't what the client is looking for. Can't you get your act together?"

"Jon, the customer is distressed with you. You really messed up this time."

"I am the one who gets paid for thinking, not you."

"You did it the wrong way again!"

"That's not the way the report is supposed to be done."

The managers didn't go beyond these statements and explain what they meant by them, add to them, or ask the staff members for their responses. They were blanket statements.

These are examples of the first type of feedback that managers use in the workplace: negative feedback. Ken Blanchard, a writer of leadership books, said that negative feedback is catching people doing something wrong and letting them know that they did something wrong. It doesn't offer or ask for alternative actions. It is the way some managers get back at their staff, especially if the manager is feeling stressed, short-tempered, or time pressured.

Negative feedback should be avoided at all costs. It leads to loss of morale; resentment; and lessening of work quality, quantity, and quickness. Giving negative feedback also runs contrary to the other Platinum skills previously discussed: developing others and active listening.

Silent or No Feedback

Here's an example that illustrates the problem with silent or no feedback. Dana Lane is one of three receptionists in a law office in Chicago. Dana is responsible for answering all incoming phone calls, greeting visitors, and helping job applicants. Often, some of the partners give him work when their personal secretaries are absent or out of the office. In short, Dana is a busy person. He reports directly to Harold, the manager of human resources. Dana has been working in the law firm for almost five months but has never received any feedback, good or bad, from Harold. Dana senses or thinks he is doing well because he is still there and no one has complained directly to him about his work. But he cannot be sure because last month one of the other receptionists, whom he thought was doing very well, was asked to leave. He is worried about his own job because he isn't sure how he is doing. On several occasions, Dana has asked Harold for some direct feedback on his job performance. Harold's usual reply is, "Let's wait and see."

Dana is on the receiving end of the second type of feedback used in the workplace: silent feedback or no feedback. Here, the manager never or rarely communicates to his team members. This leaves them unsure as to how they are doing on the job. Why leave your employees unsure? Let them know. In some organizations, no news means good news; in other organizations, no news means bad news. But why be so vague? It is the responsibility of every manager to constantly give each of his team members regular feedback on job performance.

Often managers forget to give feedback because they think their team members already know when they are doing well or when there are problems. Many team members really do not know unless their managers tell them. Feedback on performance and behavior reassures team members that the work they are doing is fine and that the manager has noticed it.

Many managers, thank goodness, are forced to communicate with each of their team members at least once a year during the annual performance appraisal. I imagine that if they weren't forced to they probably would not. Many organizations have recognized managers' lack of regular feedback and require them to do semiannual or quarterly performance reviews. The best managers, regardless of how many formal feedback sessions they have to do, meet regularly with each of their staff members and give feedback informally. Many years ago, a professor at the University of Ohio, Marge Schrader, came up with the 90/90 rule. She said that to be an effective manager, one needs to spend a minimum of 90 minutes per quarter (one minute per day) with each staff member giving feedback on the individual's job performance.

At many of the divisions of BellSouth, AT&T, and General Motors, managers have a five-minute-per-week feedback session with each of their staff members. Many other managers do not have the luxury of having their staff located near them. In that case, a phone call or e-mail is a necessary alternative.

So far, we have reviewed two types of feedback: negative and silent. Both should be avoided. Let's now look at the third type: unrelated positive feedback. Managers should steer clear of this form of feedback as well.

Unrelated Positive Feedback

When managers give feedback, the feedback should be related to their team member's job performance or work behaviors or habits. Feedback should never be given on nonwork-related issues or subjects, even if it is positive feedback. When managers do this, they may be crossing the line between doing their jobs and getting too personal. In our legally minded society and workplaces it is wise to keep away from unrelated positive feedback. Also, when managers give unrelated positive feedback in the course of talking about a work-related issue, the team member will tend to focus only on the unrelated positive feedback and not the issue at hand. Here are some examples of managers giving unrelated positive feedback to their team members. These examples come from actual companies that I've observed over the years:

> Example A: "Sally, you look great. That dress looks good on you. I hope our clients can keep their minds on the business at hand and not that dress."

> Example B (sent by e-mail): "Bob, you look like you have been working out. You must have dropped about twenty pounds. I can see your hamstrings and deltoids. Keep up the good work."

Example C (not done in private): "It is so nice to have you working with us, Christina. You are so different from the rest of the staff. I have noticed you read a lot on your breaks. It is so nice to have someone working for me who has a brain."

Example D (amid a discussion on plant safety procedures and in front of other staff members): "I forgot to tell you last week how well-behaved your kids were at last month's outing. They were the only ones who didn't seem to get into any mischief."

Example E (at a morning briefing on recent sales declines): "I would like to welcome Wong to our sales staff. I've heard great things about his golf game. That should help us snag some new clients."

The next two types of feedback, positive and constructive, are the only ones that managers should use at work.

Positive Feedback

Positive feedback is letting team members know what they did right and how it has positively influenced the work environment. Providing positive feedback correctly is valuable because it can increase employees' confidence and improve their performance. It should only take seconds to give someone positive feedback and can be done face-to-face (the best method) or by phone, e-mail, or even fax. Here are four examples:

"Leyta, staying late last week to finish the SJ project got the deliverable out on time. The customer was very pleased, and we can be assured of a renewal of the contract."

"Great report, Ted. I really like it."

"James, sharing your knowledge about the working of the KIT formula will allow Deidre to continue your work while you are away. We will be able to get the formula out to the drug company sooner than expected."

"Andersen, I was impressed with the analysis of numbers on the Reiner portfolio. You explained the statistics so well in the written report. I'm sure Mr. Reiner will be able to make an informed decision because of the quality of the information you provided. You helped this company meet its mission of satisfying customer needs."

Actually, one of these examples isn't a good example of positive feedback. It is the second one. While the manager is telling Ted something positive (i.e., he likes Ted's report), Ted may not be able to repeat the good performance because he may not know exactly what was great about the report. The manager should have said, "Ted, your report was concise, well researched and documented. The client now understands why they should invest with us. Our revenues will increase by at least 10 percent." When giving positive feedback, specifics should be mentioned (as they were in the other examples). Then employees will be motivated to repeat the positive behaviors. Some tips for giving positive feedback follow.

Be Timely. Giving someone positive feedback should be done as soon after the event as possible. It is best to give the positive feedback within days. Once a manager says something like "Remember last year when you . . . ," the positive feedback loses its conviction and importance. Additionally, the manager loses credibility and the trust of the team member.

Be Specific. If managers want certain behaviors repeated, they need to be very specific in the type of positive feedback they give. The more detailed the manager is, the more likely the behavior or action will be repeated. Managers should avoid general statements like "Nice job," "Good to have you around," or "You did excellent work on that project." In the previous examples, examples 1, 3, and 4 are very specific.

Describe the Impact. Most team members like to know how their work ties into the bigger picture or the larger scheme of things, such as meeting the goals of the unit, department, or organization. Including this impact statement makes the positive feedback even more meaningful. Here is an example (in italics) of attaching an impact statement to the positive feedback: "Cynthia, we were able to sell the client the new prototype because your field analysis convinced them that they would make money. *This met the department's goal of* *selling three new prototypes this year."* The previously given examples 1, 3, and 4 all have impact statements:

Example 1: *We can be assured of a renewal of the contract.*

Example 3: *We will be able to get the formula out to the drug company earlier than expected.*

Example 4: *You helped this company meet its mission of satisfying all customer needs.*

Avoid Assigning More Work. When managers give their team members positive feedback, they should not give them more work, especially the same type of work, at the same time. Otherwise, team members may feel they are being punished for doing well.

Don't Overdo It. Too many managers go to extremes when they give positive feedback. They give their team members too much positive feedback. When this occurs, the impact of the important feedback is diminished. I used to work with a manager who gave his team positive feedback if they showed up, came to a meeting, or came back from lunch on time. That's overdoing it. Save positive feedback for those times when employees have really done something outstanding or have improved their performance or behavior.

Keep the Message Pure. I have worked with some managers who find it very difficult to give someone only positive feedback. They have this need or habit of attaching a criticism to the message. For example, "Vincent, I want to congratulate you on such an excellent presentation on our new mobile line. The audience recognized all the new features and how those features will be of benefit. I am sure we will sell millions. But, when you run your staff meetings, you have a tendency to . . ." As soon as the manager mentions that "but" word, she has contaminated the positive message. The team member will only remember what was said after the "but" or believe that to be the more important part of the message. Managers need to separate the positive message from the constructive feedback.

Keep the Message Congruent. As mentioned in Chapter 5 on active listening, when managers send messages to their staff the message has to be congruent. The verbal, visual, and vocal components of the message have to be in sync. If a manager is giving a staff member positive feedback but his tone of voice doesn't reflect that, or if he has an unhappy look on his face, then the message is incongruent and the staff member will be confused about how to interpret the message.

Avoid the Excuses for Not Giving Positive Feedback. In many organizations, managers are hesitant to give positive feedback. They do not see their managers or their colleagues giving it, so they don't either. Effective managers need to break this cycle and give their team positive feedback when they deserve it. Giving positive feedback is quick, easy to do, and doesn't cost anything. It is a great business strategy. Positive feedback builds trust and a constructive working relationship between manager and team member. It is also one of the best motivators. Positive feedback has a ripple effect. When a manager gives someone positive feedback it makes that person feel good. When people feel good, they treat others better and often take the time to praise someone else. Many managers find many reasons for not giving positive feedback. Some of these reasons are valid; others are just excuses.

Valid Reasons

1. *"It takes time."* The benefits are, however, well worth the time investment. It should only take a minute or less to give someone some positive praise.

2. *"I'm not sure how to do it"* or *"It feels uncomfortable."* Giving positive feedback is definitely a skill that needs to be practiced (steps for giving positive feedback are described later in this section).

3. *"I have a very large staff. It is not possible to give everyone positive feedback."* Once again, it takes some time to give positive feedback, but giving praise increases productivity and profitability. Managers must make the time to praise.

Excuses

1. *"If I praise others I will be considered weak."* Quite the oppo-

site is true. It takes great strength to give others positive feedback.

2. *"I have productivity stage 5 staff. They are all great perform-ers. They don't need positive feedback."* All staff members, regardless of their productivity level, need positive feed-back. If managers do not give productivity stage 5 staff praise, they run the risk of having these staff members regress to a lower productivity stage or leave the company. Even if staff members already know that they are doing excellent work, occasionally, they need to hear it from their managers.

3. *"I have several productivity stage 2 and 3 employees. What could I possibly give them positive feedback for?"* Managers genuinely need to praise employees who deserve the recog-nition and not make it up. With employees who are not per-forming at their peak, praise should be given for any signif-icant improvements in performance or behavior.

4. *"My team will laugh at me. They'll say, 'Show me the money.'"* As we will discuss in Chapter 7 on motivation, team mem-bers definitely like tangible rewards for achieving their goals. But the majority of employees also welcome sincere verbal or written praise from their managers. In fact, praise motivates team members for much longer periods than do tangible rewards like bonuses.

Make It Private (and Maybe Public). Management circles dis-agree as to whether positive feedback should be given in private or made public. I believe both avenues are appropriate. I always recom-mend that managers give the positive feedback in private. Then, depending on the team member involved and other circumstances, decide whether to give it in public as well. Many team members don't like to get public recognition. They may feel embarrassed or don't want to be singled out if they work in a team environment. A good strategy is to consult with the team member who you are about to give public recognition to. Ask for her thoughts or permission. By the way, a great tactic for giving positive feedback is to put it in writing and place a copy in the team member's personnel file, and then send a copy to the "big" boss. Employees love this.

If a manager is thinking of giving positive feedback in front of others he should know the makeup of his group. Will there be some employees who will get jealous or feel that they should have gotten recognized as well? Will one or two people in attendance sit back and think, "Well, I did that same thing a few weeks ago and no one noticed and gave me praise for it." On the other hand, public recognition can be a great team builder and energize the entire group.

Remember That Giving Positive Feedback Is a Skill. It takes some time and practice to recognize when to give someone positive feedback and actually how to do it. Let's review the steps involved:

> Step 1: Specifically describe the behavior or performance that deserves positive feedback.
>
> *Example*: "I like the videotapes you have selected for the patient waiting area."
>
> Step 2: Describe why the behavior or performance deserves positive feedback.
>
> *Example*: "The patients will now have something to do while they wait for their doctor."
>
> Step 3: Describe the impact of the behavior or performance.
>
> *Example*: "Patients will be much more relaxed and view our medical center as one that cares about patient needs."

Managers who are not familiar with or lack experience in giving positive feedback should do some planning before they deliver positive feedback. Answering the following questions will be good preparation:

Positive Feedback Planning Guide

> ✔ What is the event or behavior that deserves the positive feedback?
>
> ✔ What are the specific behaviors that need to be acknowledged or reinforced by the positive feedback? (What type of performance do you want more of?)
>
> ✔ Is the positive feedback related to the performance of a new task

or assignment, or to the improved performance of existing tasks/assignments?

✔ Are you going to praise the person publicly or privately?

✔ In your opinion, will the person be glad to get the positive feedback? If not, why do you think so? Is there anything else you can do to show that you recognize the performance, besides giving positive feedback?

✔ Were there any other people involved who deserve positive feedback?

Constructive Feedback/Coaching

Giving positive feedback, once mastered, is one of the most valuable skills a manager has to motivate staff to high levels of performance. However, when team members are experiencing performance or behavior problems, managers need to act quickly and provide constructive feedback in order to allow team members to continue their progress.

Giving constructive feedback, sometimes referred to as coaching, involves the general communication skills of commenting, clarifying, and committing. These skills are called the 3Cs.

✔ *Commenting* is letting your team member know that some aspect of her performance or behavior is not what it should be. During their careers, managers will have to deal with many types of performance and behavior issues. Performance issues relate to team members not meeting goals or not doing what is delineated in their job descriptions. Behavioral concerns refer more to company rules and regulations and accepted codes of behavior. Examples of *performance problems* include missing deadlines, having an excessive error rate, not sharing relevant information with others, producing less than expected, or not following designated procedures. Examples of *behavior problems* include time abuse issues (e.g., lateness, excessive absences, doubling break time, missing in action), using abusive language, dressing inappropriately, or belittling other team members.

The majority of performance and behavior issues will come from team members who are at the lower productivity stages (e.g., getting attention and flying blind). However, managers should expect them from employees at any productivity stage, even stage 5 performers. Most managers I have worked with prefer to coach people with performance problems as opposed to behavioral ones. They feel, rightly, that behavioral issues often reflect the personality of the team member. And, as we know, it is very hard to change personality. Also, performance issues seem to be easier to document. However, as a manager, you will need to give team members constructive feedback on both.

✔ *Clarifying* is stating the impact of the performance or behavior problem and, as we discussed in Chapter 5 on active listening, making sure the team member understands what the problem is.

✔ *Committing* is getting your team members to take action to change what they are currently doing in order to achieve positive results.

The Roger/Alberto Case

Let's listen in to an exchange between Roger, the manager, and Alberto, the employee, as Roger spots Alberto in the company cafeteria.

Roger: I was glad to see you at yesterday's planning meeting. I know you have a very busy schedule. When can I take a look at the strategic plan that you said you would have ready last week?

Alberto: Well, Roger, I didn't get it completed. I do apologize. I just couldn't find the time to do it.

Roger: I know all about your busy schedule. Mine is just as busy, probably more so. Let me get straight to the point. I need that plan and I need it yesterday. No further discussion! This isn't some sort of hand-holding experience. Either you get it to me or I will do it myself, and you know what that would mean.

Alberto: I can't understand why you are being so tough on me. I'm working on so many projects, more than anyone else on the team. I just don't have the time to complete all of them on time. You are definitely picking on me.

Roger: You don't know what you are talking about! (yelling)

Alberto: Yes, I do! (yelling even louder)

This scenario is not what constructive feedback is about. The manager needs to remain calm and constructive, listen to the team member, and focus on resolving the issue at hand. None of this happened in this exchange. It is also the responsibility of the person receiving the constructive feedback to remain calm and constructive, listening to the person giving the feedback and working toward a joint solution. These points will be emphasized later in this chapter.

Let's now replay the scene and see how it should be done. Let's begin where Roger, the manager, is talking about busy schedules.

Roger: I'm aware of your busy schedule. I understand how difficult it must be for you to complete all of your assignments on time. What ideas do you have on how you can get to complete everything?

Alberto: I appreciate your understanding, but everyone expects me to do everything perfectly on time. It's impossible.

Roger: It may be impossible as it is now. What ideas do you have so that you could handle all these projects well? As you know, I cannot take any of them away from you at this time.

Alberto: I've been thinking that about 30 percent of each of these projects involves rudimentary paperwork. Perhaps the paperwork can be computerized, or we can get someone from the office pool to take it on.

Roger: Those are both excellent ideas. The second idea is out because I just received an e-mail from Terry (the CEO) stating that the office pool, for governmental funding purposes, can't be assigned to any of our projects. However, I see no reason why we can't computerize all those forms that have to be completed. I know what you're going through. I used to dread filling them out as well.

> *Alberto:* Do you think you can set up a meeting ASAP with Carlos (the IT director)?
>
> *Roger:* I'll try to set it up for the end of the day. I'll let you know if he's available.

The major difference in this exchange is that there's no management blaming going on, only problem solving. Managers need to view a constructive feedback session as a way to solve a problem and further build a strong manager–team member relationship. As a manager, you are not out to get the team member. It is not your chance to stab him with a dagger. It is so much easier to resolve the situation at hand instead of getting into arguments or conflicts where you may wind up having to go through the company's discipline procedure.

When Not to Give Constructive Feedback. Giving a team member constructive feedback under any of the following circumstances invariably has adverse effects:

1. *When the employee cannot take any action on the constructive feedback.* Consider the case of Kelly Sinclair. Kelly works for a chain of discount stores in the St. Louis area. He is in the marketing department. One of his responsibilities is to go to all five stores and share the latest marketing strategies with the store managers and sales staff. Last week Kelly's boss gave him some constructive feedback that Kelly could not act on. The boss said, "Kelly, I observed your presentation last week and I liked it a lot. I have one suggestion for making it even more effective. I'd like you to do the presentations in PowerPoint. The staff will be even more impressed than they are now." Unfortunately, Kelly doesn't know PowerPoint; he doesn't have a laptop computer or the PowerPoint software. The organization doesn't own an LCD projector, either. When managers provide constructive feedback and the staff member cannot do anything with that feedback, two things occur. First, the staff member becomes frustrated. He wants to do what the manager suggests but has no control over the situation. Second, the manager loses credibility in the eyes of the staff member. The man-

ager is viewed as someone who doesn't know what he is talking about.

2. *When the person giving the constructive feedback is over-stressed or has a limited amount of time.* Managers need to remain calm during feedback sessions. Once managers lose their temper, become angry, or yell, the feedback loses its impact because the person receiving the feedback has shut down and is no longer listening. When giving constructive feedback, the manager needs to listen to employees to get their perspective on the situation and to have them take ownership of the resolution. If a manager is time pressured, this dialogue won't be able to take place or employees will be shortchanged and get the sense that the manager isn't really interested in listening. It is best for managers to be in a positive frame of mind with a window of time before they attempt to provide constructive feedback.

3. *When the focus in on the person, not the person's behavior or performance.* As managers, when we give constructive feedback, our intention is to modify a team member's performance or behavior. It's a big mistake to focus on trying to change someone's personality. Psychologists tell us that personality is formed in youth and is very difficult to change. Also, managers are not qualified to change an employee's personality. The best we can hope for is to change performance and behavior. For example, let's take the case of a receptionist who answers the phone by saying, "Yeah, what do you want?" Not only are the words inappropriate, but the receptionist's vocal tone and quality may be, too. As the manager, I would want to find out why the person is answering the phone that way. Is there something on his mind that he wants to talk about? The manager's ultimate goal should be to get the receptionist to answer the phone by saying, "Good morning, SJS Industries. How may I help you?"

When giving constructive feedback, managers also want to keep away from "you" statements that put the emphasis on the personality and not the behavior or performance. For example, "You are a late person," or "You have a sloppy work area," or "You don't know how to get along with our clients."

It is much better to say, "I need to discuss the lateness record," or "I want to talk about how the work area needs to be maintained," or "Let's discuss how to improve working relationships with our clients."

4. *When previous attempts at providing constructive feedback have not worked.* If a manager has given constructive feedback on separate occasions and the behavior or performance issue still exists, the manager has to change her strategy. Continuing to give additional constructive feedback won't remedy the situation. The manager may need to get feedback from her mentor or a trusted colleague to make sure she is giving constructive feedback in the proper manner. Or the manager has to determine if the employee can act on the constructive feedback, or decide if the employee has the skill set or knowledge to do what's needed. If the employee lacks the right skill set, then he needs additional training. Or, perhaps, it is a poor job fit. If that's the case, another position needs to be found for the individual.

When previous attempts at giving constructive feedback have not worked, the manager may have no other choice but to follow the company's discipline procedure. Managers need to be supportive and try to constructively "fix" all problems. However, there are times when a more direct message of accountability needs to be sent to the team member. Discipline procedures vary from company to company. It is important for managers to familiarize themselves with their company's discipline procedures.

Recommended Steps for Delivering Constructive Feedback. Managers often miss opportunities to provide constructive feedback. They fear that giving team members anything other than positive feedback could harm their relationship. Actually, delaying or not giving constructive feedback will do more harm than good. The consequences of the uncorrected behavior or performance can begin to escalate. Employees may also begin to resent the manager for not helping them. And, most important, employees don't have the chance to improve and work toward meeting their goals and the goals of the organization. The following six steps are recommended for delivery of constructive feedback:

1. *Specifically state what you have observed and its impact.*

Being specific avoids having to have the team member guess where you are heading. It also saves time. Just as with positive feedback, be timely. Give the feedback as soon after you have become aware that there is a performance or behavior issue. If the manager waits too long to give feedback, the team member may think nothing is wrong or that the issue wasn't important since the manager waited so long to comment. The impact describes why the issue needs to be discussed in the first place. The impact should always be a business one—losing business, getting customer complaints, lessening of work quality, losing company image, etc. Team members will be more accepting of the issue if they see how it is impacting the business.

2. *Listen to the team member.* If you know what is going on and what has to be done, why should a manager go through this step? Sometimes managers are wrong. When managers provide an opportunity for responses, they learn valuable information and foster open communication. I recall an instance where a manager gave a team member feedback for not passing her report on to another team member in a timely manner. It turned out the manager's boss was asking this team member to do some tasks for her. That's why she was falling behind in her report writing.

Another reason for listening to the team member is that people like to be listened to. It motivates them and builds trust. Also, the team member may acknowledge the problem and take responsibility for it. In that case, the rest of the constructive feedback session will be a breeze. Allowing team members the chance to react to the manager's feedback builds their self-esteem and shows that the manager recognizes the value of his team's ideas or suggestions. It is also possible that the team member may try to deflect the criticism, saying, "I don't think so. I always share information in a timely manner. The rest of the team loves me. We get along wonderfully." If something like this happens (and it sometimes will), the manager has to be prepared with examples to back up her points. The manager should also have documentation, if possible, and come up with ways to "fix" the situation if the team member cannot come up with any. The manager needs to do preparation before speaking with the individual.

3. *Try to get an agreement that a problem exists.* It is always best if the team member can agree that she needs to change her behavior or improve her performance. Getting the willing cooperation of the team member makes the constructive feedback session much easier.

4. *Ask the team member what should be done to rectify the situation.* If the team member comes up with the action plan for resolving the situation at hand, he will more likely do it than if the manager tells him what needs to be done. Most of the time team members at productivity stages 3, 4, and 5 will have an answer. Managers may have to work with team members at productivity stages 1 and 2 to help them see what needs to be done. If the team member doesn't know what to do to rectify a problem or is not in a cooperative mood, the manager needs to offer solutions.

5. *Decide on what the action plan will be.* Preferably, the manager will agree with the team member's suggestion. If he cannot, the manager needs to explain why and then probe and discuss the matter further until the team member comes up with an acceptable action plan. If this cannot be done, then the manager takes charge and decides on what the action plan will be.

6. *Monitor and follow through.* Many managers believe their job is done once they have communicated the issue to the team member and the action plan has been decided on. Not quite. In a way, the manager's job has just begun. The manager needs to make sure that the performance or behavior is improving. If it is, then the manager should give positive feedback and encourage the team member to continue to improve. If the performance or behavior does not change, the manager needs to have another one or two constructive feedback sessions. If those sessions fail to bring the results the manager needs, she has to follow the discipline guidelines of her company (when previous attempts at providing constructive feedback have not worked).

Now that the steps for delivering constructive feedback have been reviewed, let's look at them in action.

The Giselle Davenport Case

Mary is a manager in a medium-size training company, Dynamic, Inc., in New York City. The firm specializes in all types of computer training. It sends trainers to company sites. One of the trainers is Giselle. Giselle has been with Dynamic Inc. for over three years. She is considered one of the firm's best trainers. She is knowledgeable in the systems she teaches, has a great training style, and receives very high marks from trainees on the feedback forms they fill out after the training sessions. Giselle averages 9.6 on a scale of 10, the best average of all the computer trainers at Dynamic. (She is probably at productivity stage 5.)

Like other trainers, Giselle usually spends about three hours at a company site per day for a period of about a month and then moves on to other organizations. Currently, Giselle is working with three different organizations. Typically, she trains nine to twelve people at a time.

In the last couple of weeks, Mary has been receiving complaints from the clients about Giselle. They say Giselle often disappears from the training room for up to sixty minutes at a time, one-third of the training period. Their concerns are that sometimes there are systems problems that only Giselle knows how to fix; when she is absent, the trainees have no one to answer their questions. The clients don't mind when she leaves for ten minutes, but an hour is unacceptable. Mary has never received any complaints from clients about Giselle in the two years she has been managing her. She has only received accolades. Mary needs to rectify this situation and find out from Giselle what's happening. She asks Giselle to stop in the office in the morning before going on to one of her company sites. Mary has arranged to meet with Giselle in the company's conference room. After a few pleasantries, Mary begins the constructive feedback session, following the recommended steps. The dialogue between Mary, the manager, and Giselle, her employee, proceeds as follows:

Step 1: Specifically State What You Have Observed and Its Impact

Mary: Giselle, I believe we may have a time issue on our hands. It's been brought to my attention in the last two weeks, from the clients whom you are currently assigned to, that the trainees are often left on their own in the training room without the assistance they need. The clients have said that sometimes the trainees are left alone for up to one hour, which is almost a third of the training time. We always want to provide a full training session and maintain excellent relationships with our clients. That makes good business sense. Our clients expect excellent service each and every time. And you have always done this. Can you tell me what's going on? I'm perplexed. Any ideas?

Step 2: Listen to the Team Member

Giselle: It's so strange that the clients are saying that. I cannot imagine why. As you know, I often leave the training room for five or ten minutes to take a break, but no way is it for an hour. I have no idea why they have said this. In the three years I have been working here, I have never received any kind of complaint.

Mary: When I first heard the complaint I couldn't imagine it myself. You have consistently been our top performer for the last three years. You've been a role model for the other computer trainers. Can you think of any reasons why all of these clients have told me the same thing? I'm certain it's nothing against you, because they have always told us at Dynamic Inc. that they only want you as the trainer.

Giselle: I'm dumbfounded. I just can't imagine that I am ever out of the room for more than ten minutes, maybe fifteen, tops. And I do such a great job.

Mary: Do you think that it is possible that it's really longer than fifteen minutes?

Giselle: It's possible, but I am so conscientious about my work that I cannot imagine it to be as long as that.

Step 3: Try to Get an Agreement That a Problem Exists

Mary: The clients insist that it is about an hour. I guess we can agree that we do have a problem here, at least between what you and they are telling me?

Giselle: Don't you believe me?

Mary: Giselle, I believe you. And I need to believe what the clients are telling me as well.

Step 4: Ask the Team Member What Should Be Done to Rectify the Situation

Mary: So what do you think we can do about this discrepancy?

Giselle: I guess I better monitor my break time. I need to get myself a watch and monitor my time much closer. I'll also tell the trainees that I will be out for five or ten minutes. But I still cannot believe that I am out of the training room for up to an hour. It's just impossible.

Mary: These are excellent ideas. Anything else going on that you want to talk about?

Giselle: No, I think that will do the trick.

Step 5: Decide on What the Action Plan Will Be

Mary: Then we are in agreement. You'll wear a watch from now on and monitor your time when you take your breaks. You will also inform the trainees when you are leaving the room for a five- or ten-minute break. I'm sure that this action plan will work well. I'm looking forward to putting this incident behind us.

Giselle: No problem. I'm looking forward to it as well.

Step 6: Monitor and Follow Through

A few days later Mary received calls from Giselle's clients. They said that the out-of-the-room behavior persisted and that the trainees were now beginning to complain. Mary had several more constructive feedback sessions with Giselle, and Giselle stuck to her guns at these sessions. She said that her breaks were only ten minutes and that she was checking her watch to make sure. Then Mary began to get the same feedback about Giselle from the new clients Giselle was assigned to. Mary had additional constructive feedback sessions where she was much more directive. She told Giselle exactly what was expected of her. She told Giselle that she had to follow Dynamic Inc.'s regulations concerning break time and put Giselle on a performance improvement plan.

Mary also offered Giselle the opportunity to speak to someone at an employee assistance program that Dynamic Inc. had arranged for. Giselle refused, stating that the clients didn't know what they were talking about.

Epilogue

Unfortunately, Giselle's behavior never changed. In fact, it got worse. Sometimes she would never return to the training room. These absences began to seriously affect her performance and her ratings slipped dramatically. The clients refused to accept Giselle as the trainer. Giselle, however, kept to the same story.

Eventually, Mary had to have Giselle return to the home office, where she was given other projects to do. Giselle continued her pattern of disappearing for excessive amounts of time at the home office as well. Eventually, Giselle was terminated. Mary never did find out before she terminated Giselle what was really happening.

This case demonstrates the steps involved in delivering constructive feedback. A manager should be supportive and listen to the ideas of the team member. This approach usually rectifies the situation. However, if the performance or behavior under question does not change, the manager needs to remind the team member of the goal and hold the team member accountable.

Additional Tips for Giving Constructive Feedback

1. When giving constructive feedback, avoid a laundry list. Deal with one issue at a time. More than one at a time can become overwhelming and have a negative effect instead of the positive effect intended.

2. Select a time when the team member is likely to be most receptive. Avoid times when the team member is busy, upset, or about to leave for the day.

3. Only give constructive feedback in private. It is best to deliver constructive feedback face-to-face.

4. Be aware of your own shortcomings. Have you prepared enough? Are you trying to rush through the meeting? Do you have problems being a good listener? Do you want to decide on the action plan on your own? Are you willing to do the follow-up?

5. Remember the impact that visual and vocal communications have—be congruent.

6. Don't assume that team members who are at a high productivity stage can always solve their own problems or are always aware that they have a performance or behavior issue. It is imperative for the manager to give the feedback and to give these team members the support and/or the direction that they need.

How to Receive Feedback

The other half of feedback that managers need to be concerned about is being able to successfully handle the feedback that team members or others give them. Managers need to view receiving feedback as a plus. If a team member is willing to give a manager feedback, it demonstrates that the team member is concerned about meeting the goals of the department or organization. It shows that the team member cares. It also demonstrates that the manager has built a relationship with her team where issues and problems can be talked about openly. Just like employees, managers often are not aware that certain actions of theirs are causing concerns.

The more typical concerns for which team members give their managers feedback are:

- ✔ Not sharing information
- ✔ Not involving the team member in decisions
- ✔ Bypassing the team member and going directly to the team member's direct employee (if the team member has supervisory responsibilities)
- ✔ Taking credit for the accomplishment of a team member
- ✔ Not giving team members the opportunities for growth and development that they are looking for
- ✔ Micromanaging
- ✔ Giving unclear or nonspecific directions
- ✔ Being vague in the feedback given (e.g., "The client is complaining about the service he is getting")
- ✔ Being biased or making decisions based on assumptions

The Four Ways to Respond to Constructive Feedback

There are four ways that managers react to constructive feedback. Read the following scenarios and then select your answer to determine the way you prefer to receive feedback.

Scenario 1. You are given constructive feedback for something you definitely didn't do. You decide to:

- a. Defend yourself by saying, "I did not do that."
- b. Blame the team member for not knowing what he was saying.

    c. Avoid the feedback and not respond.

    d. Ask the team member to give his rationale for saying what he did.

Scenario 2. An angry team member comes into your office and says that you aren't managing him or other team members correctly. You:

    a. Tell the team member that you are a great manager and he must be confused.

    b. Tell the team member that if he were a better employee, there would be no problems.

    c. Just laugh and go about your business.

    d. Ask the team member to explain what he and others need from you that they are not getting.

Scenario 3. A customer gives you feedback that the company's product is unacceptable. You:

    a. Tell the customer that your company has the best product, better than all of the competition.

    b. Tell the customer to get her facts right and to call back when she does.

    c. Refer the call to someone else.

    d. Ask the customer for specifics about what she expected that she did not get.

The four ways to receive feedback are protecting, attacking, avoiding, and improving:

   ✔ *Protecting.* When a team member gives a manager some feedback and the manager becomes defensive or denies the statement, then the manager is being protective. Being protective is not the proper way to respond to feedback. It sends a message to the team member that the manager is not open to listening to constructive feedback. In the previous scenarios, if you answered "a," you gave protecting answers.

✔ *Attacking.* When the manager blames the team member who is giving the feedback, the manager is attacking. Attacking behavior will cause team members never to give their managers constructive feedback and cause a breakdown in the manager-employee relationship. If you answered "b" in the previous situations, you were attacking.

✔ *Avoiding.* When a manager avoids the feedback by not responding to it, she is escaping from the situation. This type of reaction will cause team members to discount the manager's commitment to her job. The team members will lose trust and loyalty. Answering "c" in any of the previous situations indicates you are avoiding.

✔ *Improving.* This is the way a manager should respond to constructive feedback. Here, the manager is trying to clarify what the team member has said and is open to discussing the feedback. The manager is not automatically admitting that she was wrong but showing the team member that through dialogue, they will be able to resolve the situation. Answers "d" were improving responses.

How did you score? What is your preferred way of receiving feedback?

Tips for Receiving Feedback

1. Take in the team member's point of view. Let the individual vent frustrations.

2. Suspend the urge to attack or counterattack.

3. Remain calm. Don't get caught up in your emotions or the emotions of the team member.

4. Ask questions to find out more of what the team member is saying.

5. Acknowledge what the team member is saying or feeling.

6. Thank the team member for her input or opinion.

7. Find some common ground—something specific you can agree on.

8. Clarify to make sure you have understood what the team member has said and to let her know that you have understood her.

9. Maintain eye contact, a moderate tone of voice, and appropriate facial expressions.

Responding to Valid, Invalid, or Unclear Feedback

It's also important to recognize that there are different types of feedback, each of which requires a different response.

Valid Feedback. Valid constructive feedback is in some ways the most difficult type of feedback for managers to handle. Valid feedback means that the feedback is accurate and the team member is correct.

The best way to respond to valid constructive feedback is to agree. Agreeing allows the manager to accept his mistakes and faults without apologizing for them. Sample responses might be to say:

> "You are right. I didn't take the time to ask your opinion. Now I realize you could have really helped me in coming up with the best decision."

> "I agree. Holding the meeting at the end of the day did not allow for full participation. Most of the staff was anxious to leave."

Invalid Feedback. In this case the team member is wrong. She is giving feedback that's inaccurate. Perhaps she has her facts wrong, is in an angry or distressed mood, or has a perception of the situation that is not accurate. The manager can respond in two ways. If the manager feels the team member is calm and willing to listen, he can explain the facts and clear up any misunderstandings. If the team member is in a highly emotional state and the manager knows that this isn't the best time to explain the facts, he needs to "fog" the team member.

Fogging is calm acknowledgment of the possibility that there may be some truth in the constructive feedback. When the manager fogs, he prevents the exchange from going any further. When the team member has calmed down, he can discuss the constructive criticism. Here are a couple of examples:

Invalid feedback:	"You always come late to the meetings you scheduled."
Fogging response:	"It is very important to come to meetings on time."
Invalid feedback:	"Every time you are told about an error, you get defensive."
Fogging response:	"You might be right about my tendency to get defensive. I don't like it when I make errors."

When you fog, you do not apologize or admit guilt. You are trying to stop the emotional reaction of the team member.

Unclear Feedback. When the feedback is vague, the manager really doesn't know what the team member intended. The feedback is not specific enough. Examples of unclear feedback are when someone on your team says:

"You are not much of a team player, are you?"

"You are not managing us like your predecessor did."

When the manager gets this vague type of constructive feedback, she needs to request specifics. The manager should respond by asking a question: "Can you give me some examples of how I have not been a team player?" or "Exactly how did my predecessor manage the department?"

Chapter Summary

The third of our four Platinum skills is giving and receiving feedback. When managers give feedback, there are only two forms to use: positive and constructive. Silent, negative, and unrelated positive feedback should all be avoided. When giving a team member positive feedback, managers need to be timely and specific, maintain congruence, and describe the positive business impact the team member's performance or behavior has had. Some managers find excuses not to give positive feedback, but they need to understand that positive feedback is one of the best ways to build a motivated team. (Chapter 7 further examines the last of the Platinum skills: motivating.)

When team members are experiencing performance or behavior problems managers need to give them constructive feedback. There are six steps to delivering constructive feedback. The steps are to (1) specifically describe the issue and its impact, (2) listen to the response of the team member, (3) agree that a problem exists, (4) ask the team member for a solution or action plan, (5) agree on an action plan, and (6) monitor and follow up.

Finally, there are three different strategies managers have for responding to the feedback that they receive from their team members: to agree, to fog, or to ask for specifics. Your role as the manager is to determine what type of feedback it is and to respond appropriately. If the team member is giving you feedback and he is accurate, admit that the feedback is valid. If the team member is unable to calmly talk about the situation, neutralize the situation by fogging. And if the team member is being unspecific with the feedback, request more information in order to clarify what the team member actually meant.

CHAPTER 7

The Platinum Skill of Creating a Motivational Climate

Can a manager really motivate team members? No, a manager cannot motivate other people. People can only motivate themselves. What a manager needs to do is to create an environment where team members will want to motivate themselves. The most successful managers find out what the needs of their team members are and then try to meet those needs. Chances are, if a manager can find out what each of his team members needs, and then help them get it, then the manager has created an environment in which team members will want to motivate themselves.

We start by looking at how managers can keep their own positive attitude in the workplace so they will be able to help create a motivational environment. Then we examine the three pieces or components that create this environment: the organization, the organization and the manager, and the manager. The chapter concludes with fifteen strategies for getting team members to motivate themselves.

The Manager's Attitude

There is a very famous quote of General Eisenhower's from World War II that sums up the type of attitude managers need to maintain in the workplace if they want to build a motivating work environment. Eisenhower said to his commanding officers in 1942 after a setback: "Without optimism, victory is scarcely obtainable."

If managers are negative or pessimistic in the workplace, then their team members will tend to be the same, and vice versa. It is the responsibility of every manager to remain as positive as possible. Most everyone would agree that team members who have a positive attitude at work perform better than those with a more pessimistic attitude.

A manager's positive attitude is extremely appreciated by team members. There are four reasons:

1. Approximately half of a person's waking hours are spent at work. Without some positive attitudes in the workplace, this amount of time would seem endless.

2. Team members depend on the positive attitude of their manager to establish a strong team spirit.

3. Some team members have difficult personal lives. Where they work can be a place to find positive people who can help them forget some of their difficulties.

4. For many team members, work is not what they would prefer to be doing. Working near a positive person makes their work more enjoyable.

Positive attitude can be broken down into eight different competencies. Take a look at the following list to see if you possess all eight of them.

The Eight Positive Attitude Competencies

1. *Optimism* is a belief in and expectation of positive outcomes, even in the face of difficulty, challenge, or crisis.

2. *Enthusiasm* means having high levels of interest, positive energy, or personal motivation.

3. *Integrity* is acting on a personal commitment to fairness and honesty.

4. *Courage* is the willingness to take risks and overcome fears, even when the outcome is uncertain.

5. *Confidence* is being personally assured of one's abilities, capabilities, and potential.

6. *Determination* is the tireless pursuit of a goal, purpose, or cause.

7. *Patience* is the willingness to wait for opportunity, readiness, or results from yourself or others.

8. *Calmness* means taking time to reflect and think.

Techniques for Maintaining a Positive Attitude

There are many ways that managers can maintain their positive attitude in the workplace. Managers can, for example:

- ✔ Set goals for themselves and accomplish those goals.

- ✔ Do an excellent job and receive positive feedback from their managers.

- ✔ Create an environment for themselves and their team members that's spontaneous and creative and where people can relax and laugh and play. The manager can keep a log or journal of her favorite jokes, and when she notices her positive attitude diminishing, she can take a look at it. Or the manager can subscribe to a joke-a-day e-mail service, or call up a friend or team member and ask them for a joke or funny story.

- ✔ Use the Platinum skills, which help managers get results and feel proud that they have done their all to develop a high-performing team.

- ✔ Keep learning new technical and managerial skills.

- ✔ Display their successes, by having awards, certificates, diplomas, pictures of loved ones in the office and looking at them throughout the day.

- ✔ Ask for or give a standing ovation. When the manager has had a tough day, is beginning to feel stressed out, or feels that positive attitude slipping away, she needs to walk around the office or plant and gather up a few team members. She needs to tell them about the deadline, the new projects assigned to the group, or the new quality requirements and say, "I have been working hard; I need a standing ovation." Asking for a standing ovation is much better than complaining or letting the tension build up. It automatically puts the manager in a positive frame of mind. Managers also need to give their team members standing ovations.

✓ Smile, because smiling makes you happier. The facial muscles that move during smiling send messages back to the brain that change the manager's mood and emotional state for the better. People who live longer tend to smile more. Team members tend to trust their smiling managers more. Smiling signifies openness and acceptance.

✓ Take a time-out. If the manager believes he is in danger of having a temporary bout of pessimism, he needs to take a time-out. He needs to remove himself from the environment or situation that's causing the loss of the positive attitude. Five or ten minutes away can do wonders and restore the manager's positive frame of mind. He can take a walk outside, go to the cafeteria for a cup of tea, or sit in an empty conference room.

✓ Use positive self-talk. Self-talk is a term for stream of consciousness thoughts or beliefs that reflect a person's attitude toward events in her life. Self-talk often makes for a self-fulfilling prophecy. It is vital that managers control what they say to themselves. By thinking positive thoughts and experiencing positive feelings about themselves, managers maintain a positive attitude that is communicated to others. Examples of positive self-talk are:

"I can get the team to finish the project on time."

"I know I can move Delia into productivity stage 5 within the next three months."

"I am really good at managing."

"I achieved a goal I never thought I would."

There are many other techniques that managers could use in addition to the ones just mentioned to maintain a positive attitude at work. Managers need to find the strategies that work for them. If managers lose their positive attitude, their team members may lose theirs as well. There is a direct correlation between a manager's positive attitude and the motivational level of his team.

Components of a Motivational Environment

There are three components—the organization, the organization and its managers, and the managers—that, when they work harmoniously, create a motivating work environment (see Figure 7-1). Motivating, as we will see, is very easy to understand but hard to implement. It is hard because it takes a commitment and partnership from both the organization and the managers to do their respective parts in cultivating an environment where team members can be motivated to develop to their fullest. If any one of these three components is not present or only partially present, it may be impossible to create that motivating environment. Let's now look at these components.

Figure 7-1. The three motivational components.

Component 1: The Organization

The organization or company has a responsibility for providing an environment where individuals can become motivated. The organization needs to:

1. Establish a secure workplace.

2. Maintain good working conditions.

3. Offer competitive salaries.

4. Have a company image that people want to be proud of.

When an organization satisfies these basic concerns that individuals have in the workplace, it has done its job in the motivational partnership. Even though the organization assumes most of the responsibility for these items, the manager does have influence.

Secure Workplace. To team members a secure workplace means job security, fringe benefits, and safety.

- ✔ *Job Security.* As much as possible, an organization needs to give team members the comfort that their jobs are secure. If a team member comes to work each day and doesn't know if he will be there next week because of downsizing or reorganization, it will be difficult for him to feel motivated. Job security is mostly in the hands of the organization, but managers can certainly influence a team member's perception of it by their acceptance or rejection of job performance. If managers document and discipline unacceptable performers and work to keep and develop good and excellent performers, they will be sending a powerful message. In addition, managers can increase job security by keeping team members updated on coming changes, and providing them with specific instructions, training, and continual feedback.

- ✔ *Fringe Benefits.* Most team members, when they are hired, expect to receive reasonable fringe benefits for the type of job that they have. They will expect to have medical coverage, hospitalization, sick days, vacation time, and even flextime or the opportunity to telecommute. If people get reasonable amounts of these fringe benefits, they will feel satisfied at work.

- ✔ *Safety.* If the people on your team are worried about how safe equipment is, or if they are breathing in some toxic air, or if they fear that an unwelcome intruder will pose a physical threat, they won't feel comfortable at work. Managers have the responsibility of making sure that their work areas are safe and reminding team members of safety procedures.

Good Working Conditions. Working conditions have to do with the availability of things such as state-of-the-art equipment, appropriate lighting, adequate parking facilities, heat in the winter and air-conditioning in the summer, comfortable chairs, a good cafeteria, and conference rooms.

When the organization invests in good working conditions it is giving the staff a message that the organization cares about them. When an organization neglects them, it opens the door for the staff to not want to be motivated. Once again, managers need to be vigilant about the working conditions in their areas and bring any problems to the attention of the organization immediately.

The Case of the Parking Dilemma

There is an organization in New Jersey that recently merged all of its sites into one. There are now about 3,000 people working at this one location. Starting time is 9:00 A.M. The organization has a huge outdoor parking lot to accommodate all of the automobiles. There is no reserved parking unless a staff member is disabled. There is a visitor's section near the entrance to the building. If a staff member gets to work later than others, he will have at least a ten- or fifteen-minute walk to the building. New Jersey is cold, snowy, and icy in the winter. In the summer it is hot and humid. One of the biggest causes of unhappiness is the parking lot. I have known of vice presidents who vie for the employees-of-the-month slots because the reward is valet parking. People resist going to meetings outside of the building because they will lose their parking space, which may be close to the building. And forget about going out to lunch!

Competitive Salaries. When they are interviewing for a job, most people know what the salary range should be for the type of position they are applying for. They have done some benchmarking with friends or relatives. If they get the job, they will expect their salary to be within that range. If it isn't, the organization has not created the type of environment where team members will be motivated. Managers can influence a team member's salary by making recommendations to their managers.

Company Image. Imagine one of your team members is sitting on an airplane coming back from a business trip. The person next to him is talking about her company and what a great place it is to work. When she asks him whom he works for, how does he reply? Does he make up a different company name, say he is a consultant, or tell her how much he likes working at your organization, in your unit or department?

If you want your team members to be motivated at work, you should care that they feel good about where they work. Companies that have good images—regarding their products or services, their community involvement, and how they treat their people—foster the team member's desire to be motivated. The manager can also influence the image that team members have of their company. The manager can be positive about the organization and speak constructively about its mission and goals.

Component 2: The Organization and Its Managers

The organization and its managers have certain joint responsibilities in motivating individuals. They have to:

1. Provide for excellent supervision.
2. Give rewards to those individuals and teams that deserve them.
3. Build social relationships among the staff.
4. Treat staff fairly.

Supervision. One of the biggest factors that adds or takes away from how motivated a team member feels at work is the individual's relationship with her immediate supervisor or manager. When surveys ask team members what motivates them the most at work, supervision is usually near the top of the list. There are many stories of team members who have had promotional opportunities or been offered higher-paying jobs in other companies but who turned down the offers because of their working relationship with, or their respect for, their immediate bosses.

The organization's responsibility for supervision is to recruit and/or promote those individuals who want to be managers and to give them all the necessary training, guidance, and mentoring to become successful at managing. The manager's responsibility is to become the best possible manager.

Rewards. We are talking here about things that have a monetary value associated with them. (Psychic rewards, like praise for a job well done, are equally important!) The monetary value can be small or large. Rewards are in addition to what the team member is already receiving and should be given for superior performance. Examples of rewards include bonuses, stock options, profit sharing, time off with pay (in addition to vacation time or holidays), dinners, lunches, use of a company car, company-sponsored picnics and outings, theater tickets, spot awards (receiving money on the spot for excellent performance), clothing, and watches.

The organization's responsibility is to adequately fund rewards (sometimes called "perks," which is shorthand for perquisite but also an appropriate name because they can perk the spirit of a team member) and to guarantee that rewards are distributed fairly. The managers' responsibility is to decide who in their unit or department meets the criteria for the reward and to see that they get the reward. The organization and its managers, working together, should decide on what the rewards should be. It is definitely a good idea to include team members in the decision about what the rewards will be.

There are a few key points to remember about rewards:

1. *Rewards are short term.* A manager cannot say, for example, "What do you mean we don't try to motivate you? Don't you remember that pizza party we had two years ago?" That won't work. Rewards work for a period of time, and then team members forget about them.

2. *Rewards have to be meaningful.* Many team members don't appreciate getting certain types of rewards because they are not meaningful to them. Not all employees like to go to the theater or dine out, or they don't need to receive another company T-shirt. Managers and organizations need to realize that what one team member considers a reward another person may not.

   One of the best ways of distributing rewards is cafeteria style, or giving staff members a choice as to the reward they want. Let's say a particular team member becomes employee of the month. Under the cafeteria plan she gets to choose what she wants from a long list of items. Following is a sampling of items that have appeared on cafeteria award lists:

- Pet-grooming services for your cat or dog
- Skydiving lessons
- Foreign language lessons
- A family portrait
- Morning coffee and treats every Friday for your team for six months
- A year's supply of M&Ms
- A day at a spa for you and your significant other
- A shopping spree at the supermarket
- Flowers delivered to your desk once a month for the next four months
- Lunch with the CEO at a restaurant of your choice
- A donation in your name to your favorite charity
- Limo pickup and return trip for one week
- Sports lessons for your child
- Two days off with pay
- A party in your honor with the entire company invited

The Basketball Game Case

In 1999, a bank in Los Angeles gave its entire staff free basketball tickets with seating in the best sections of Staples Center (the sports arena). This reward backfired on the bank and its managers because the reward tickets were to a Clipper game. In 1999, the Clippers were the worst team in the history of NBA basketball. No one was going to the games except some relatives. The banking staff didn't appreciate this reward; in fact, they became very angry and resentful when they received it. They felt as if the bank really did not care about them by rewarding them in such a way. If the bank and its managers had decided to give the staff Laker tickets, it would have been another story. Then, even if a team member didn't especially like basketball, he could have easily given the tickets away to family members, friends, or neighbors.

3. *Rewards have to be fairly distributed.* In many organizations certain individuals, teams, or departments seem to get most of the rewards or have a much better chance of getting them based on who they are and not on their performance. Managers and organizations need to have a systematic way, based on set criteria, to determine who receives the rewards. Team members from any department or holding any job title should feel that they are eligible for a reward and have an equal chance of getting it, if they do outstanding work.

4. *The ante has to be raised.* If, for example, over the last three years all productivity stage 5 team members received a 5 percent bonus, and they get another 5 percent this year, the bonus won't be as motivational as it once was. It may have to be raised to 6 percent or 7 percent. After a period of time, rewards tend to level off. If managers and organizations want to increase motivational levels, they will have to increase the amount of the reward, or replace it with a more desirable reward.

5. *Once given, rewards are hard to rescind.* Organizations and managers want to give staff rewards that they appreciate and promote a higher motivational level. That is the major purpose of giving rewards. If these rewards are then taken away or reduced, it will have a detrimental effect on the staff. It is almost better not to have given the rewards in the first place.

The Case of Fridays Off

Heather works for one of the country's larger computer manufacturers. For the last three years, the company's policy has been to give staff members every other Friday off. Several times a year this has made for some nice four-day weekends (when tied to Monday holidays). Five months ago the company changed its policy and reverted back to the five-day workweek. Heather and her colleagues were alarmed and dismayed. They couldn't believe it. They had gotten so used to this reward that when it was taken away, a steep drop in staff motivation followed. Even new staff members who came on board after the Friday policy was changed back are going around complaining about the loss.

Giving rewards is an excellent strategy for building an environment where people will feel motivated. Keep in mind that not every reward will be motivating to all team members. Managers and the organization need to determine what rewards will work best. Asking team members for their suggestions is a wise move. Rewards also have to be fairly distributed so everyone has a chance to partake in the rewards system. When the same reward is repeatedly used, it may, over time, lose its capacity to motivate. And when we take away rewards that people like, we are jeopardizing their wanting to be motivated.

Social Relationships. Most team members like to have people to talk to. They want to share their thoughts and ideas and socialize with others on the team. Most staff members want to get to know each other on a more personal level. It makes them feel more secure and fulfills people's need to belong. When organizations and managers provide social opportunities for team members, they are enhancing the chances that people will want to be motivated. There are many strategies that can be used to foster social relationships. Here are just a few ideas:

- ✔ Organize sports teams that compete against other departments or organizations.
- ✔ Make available exercise, meditation, or yoga classes.
- ✔ Hold educational seminars and workshops.
- ✔ Organize theme days, such as a bring-your-child-to-work day or pet day.

✔ Take the team out to lunch occasionally or bring in some donuts or bagels.

✔ Have places besides the cafeteria where staff members can talk comfortably.

✔ Speak to staff members and ask them what type of social activities they would prefer.

Fair Treatment. Fair treatment is an intangible motivator. It cannot be seen or purchased. However, it is real. If organizations and managers treat their team members consistently with regard to policies, standards, rules, and behaviors, they will create a workplace environment of caring. When team members feel cared for, their loyalty and trust increase. When this happens, they will want to be motivated. Team members will especially be looking for fair treatment during the *critical interventions*. Critical interventions are those occasions when the organization and its managers officially evaluate a team member's ability to do a job or task, or to move to the next level or performance proficiency. Seven critical interventions are particularly important to team members:

The Seven Critical Interventions

1. Hiring a new team member
2. Selecting an existing team member for a special project or assignment
3. Determining who should be afforded a special learning opportunity
4. Planning a team member's career path
5. Scheduling formal and informal feedback sessions, including the performance appraisal
6. Selecting a team member for promotion
7. Assigning the shift, location, department, or the manager the team member reports to

It is especially at these seven times, or the critical incidents, when organizations and managers demonstrate how fair they are really being. Managers have direct contact with team members and make most of the decisions involving the critical incidents. However, the organization needs to make sure that its managers are making the right decisions and treating all team members fairly.

Case Study: Selecting a Team Member for Promotion

After six years as a branch manager, Victoria has finally been promoted to director of operations, overseeing all twelve branches. The company prefers to fill vacancies with internal candidates, and Victoria has been asked to pick one of her current employees to replace her as branch manager.

Three of her seven employees are part-timers, while two others are recent hires. That narrows her choice down to two candidates: Joshua and Marilyn. Both have good records and both have indicated that they would welcome the promotion. Victoria knows that this isn't going to be an easy choice. To help organize her thinking, she lists the characteristics of a good branch manager and puts together some notes about both Joshua and Marilyn.

Reviewing her notes, Victoria decides that both candidates have the qualifications. They both have knowledge of the computer systems, policies, and procedures. Although Marilyn has more experience in terms of customer service, Joshua is a quick learner and beginning to excel in this area, too. He seems to have a special rapport with the customers. They both have a can-do attitude, but Joshua clearly shines in this respect. Marilyn has learned to rely on him when she needs to be away from the branch for days at a time. But Marilyn is "one of the girls," eating lunch with her colleagues and socializing with them after work. Moreover, Victoria's husband and Marilyn's boyfriend are also best buddies. Ultimately, Marilyn gets the promotion.

Has Joshua been treated fairly? Will he still want to be motivated? Should the organization agree that Marilyn was the best candidate?

Case Study: The Feedback Session

After reviewing the customer profiles of all of the automobile salespeople who directly report to her, Nadia noticed an alarming increase in the number of complaints at one of the showrooms. Nadia is responsible for half of the showrooms and forty-five salespeople.

Salespeople at the showrooms work hard and often deal with customers who have their own agendas and can be difficult at times. Customer complaints at each showroom normally average five to six per month. However, she noticed that at the Long Branch showroom, the average for last month was nineteen complaints. She investigated further and found out that one of the salespeople, Gywnn, had fifteen of the nineteen complaints filed against her. Gywnn has been with the company for twenty-five years and was considered one of the better salespeople, always earning above her quotas for the month and receiving very few customer complaints. She was recently transferred to the Long Branch location because of her more senior age. The Long Branch customers are mostly senior citizens.

Nadia remembered that Gywnn had just reached her sixty-fourth birthday and would be eligible for retirement in one year. Nadia reviewed comments from the complaint log. Words and phrases varied from complaint to complaint, but common themes were apparent: inaccurate information about automobile prices and discounts; poor listening (several customers said they felt as if they were talking to a machine); and arguments with existing customers about their service appointments and treatment at the time of service. Nadia knew she had to take action. She considered speaking to Gywnn, but decided it wouldn't do any good. It takes over a year to document and terminate an employee at the company. By then, Gywnn would have retired.

Was Nadia being fair? Was she treating Gywnn differently from any other salesperson? Should she have documented and spoken to Gywnn? How will the other salespeople react to this lack of managerial action? Did she just assume that anyone who is sixty-four years old is ready to retire?

Component 3: The Managers

Up to this point we have reviewed two of the three components for creating a motivational environment: the organization, and the organization and its managers. The organization's role in the motivation picture is to satisfy the fundamental needs of its employees; the role of the manager and the organization working together is to demonstrate that they value their employees.

For some employees this is enough. If these first two components are taken care of then these employees will be motivated. However, the vast majority of employees need something else. That something else is the responsibility of the manager and is the third component of motivation. The manager's job in motivation is to build the self-worth of the employee. Self-worth is the opinion employees have of themselves. The higher an employee's self-worth on the job, the more she will be motivated and productive. The manager needs to build self-worth in employees through:

1. Recognition of achievements
2. Independence
3. Interdependence
4. Interesting work
5. Advancement

Recognition of Achievements. Part of Chapter 6 was devoted to giving positive feedback, which is the prime way to recognize team members' achievements. There are three additional ways that managers can recognize their team members: by offering visibility, publicizing accomplishments, and exerting strong will.

  ✔   *Offering Visibility.* A manager can give a team member greater visibility by letting her make presentations (or parts of presentations) to senior management, having her attend more influential meetings, or mentioning her contributions to others in the organization.

I once worked for a manager who pulled a few strings and got our team's picture and names displayed on a local downtown billboard. That was visibility!

✔ *Publicizing Accomplishments.* When the team member achieves something that is outstanding, the manager can get it written up in the company newsletter or in a local newspaper. The manager can also notify a professional organization in the team member's field that might be willing to do a story on the accomplishments.

A manager friend of mine at Fox Studios takes her team out to lunch every few months and invites two or three senior managers to meet her team (a clever tactic because the senior manager usually expenses the lunch).

✔ *Exerting Strong Will.* The theme of *Pygmalion,* the George Bernard Shaw play that later became the musical *My Fair Lady,* is that through the power of strong will, an individual can literally transform another person. That is what Professor Higgins did with Eliza Doolittle. Managers can transform their team members as well through the power of strong will. What managers expect of their team members and the way they treat them often determines how a team member will perform.

Independence. Giving team members independence is another way that managers can create a motivating environment. Having autonomy, or freedom on the job, means being able to work on one's own without close supervision. Before a manager can give team members independence, he has to develop each individual to perform at productivity stage 5. Independence reflects the team member's need to set his own goals and targets, have ownership over his work, measure his own progress, be in control of his own behavior, be accountable for important resources, and have the authority to make decisions and solve problems on his own. There are several levels of decision making that managers use, depending on the productivity stage of the team member (see Figure 7-2). When motivating a team member by giving him independence, the decision-making level should be a level 5.

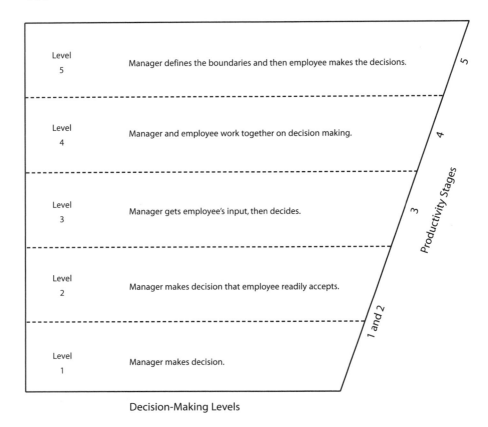

Figure 7-2. Decision-making levels and productivity stages.

Interdependence. Another responsibility of the manager is providing a motivational environment that builds team spirit, where team members rely on each other and help each other with their work products. Interdependence is not in conflict with independence. Being independent does not mean that a team member works in isolation. He needs the assistance and support of other team members in order to accomplish his goals. Interdependence is also different from social relationships. Interdependence is directly related to performing one's job effectively, whereas social relationships are about having people to be friendly with.

In order for managers to build this interdependent working relationship, they need to do the following:

✔ Let all team members know the specific goals of the team (work unit or department).

✔ Make certain that each team member understands the team's priorities and procedures.

✔ Have the team understand how it fits into the organizational mission.

✔ Have everyone on the team work toward accomplishing the goals of the team.

✔ Give feedback to team members on how they are progressing in meeting team goals.

✔ Give team members the resources needed to meet the desired outcomes.

✔ Allow team members to make decisions that affect their work.

✔ Keep all team members up-to-date about what is going on in the organization.

✔ Instill open, honest, and timely communication among team members.

✔ Make certain that all team members have the skills they need to accomplish their roles.

✔ Have all team members understand the roles and responsibilities of every other team member.

✔ Teach team members how to resolve conflicts, listen to each other, and recognize the contributions of other team members.

As a way of motivating team members by building this interdependent working atmosphere, the manager needs to make sure that the team members themselves can answer, with their other team members, questions regarding their progress. Next is a sampling of the type of questions interdependent team members ask when they are working with other interdependent team members. The questions cover four categories of interdependent behavior: interaction, function, purpose, and procedure.

1. *Interaction* includes communication, trust, support, friendliness, feedback, and satisfaction. The questions interdependent team members need to ask are:

   a. What is the quality of our interactions?

   b. Do we give personal and task-related feedback?

   c. Are there underlying conflicts that are not addressed?

   d. How open are we with each other?

   e. Do we trust each other and how do we demonstrate that trust?

   f. Do we share our perceptions about each other?

   g. How satisfied are we with working together?

   h. Are we sensitive to all team members' feelings and how do we show that we are?

   i. Have we been sure to include everyone in the team, in order to develop a sense of belonging?

   j. Do we work together with conviction, excitement, and enthusiasm?

2. *Function* includes job content, roles and responsibilities, use of resources, participation, involvement, and control. The questions interdependent team members need to ask are:

   a. Do we know what tasks we need to accomplish?

   b. Do we know which team members should be doing what?

   c. How are we interdependent with each other?

   d. How should we work with each other to get the job done?

   e. How can we best coordinate our efforts?

   f. Have we organized our tasks and roles appropriately?

   g. Have we built in the necessary checks and balances?

   h. Do we know who is accountable for what?

   i. Who is going to take the lead in which areas?

   j. How will we keep ourselves on track? How will our progress be monitored?

3. *Purpose* includes the clarification of mission, plans, and priorities. The questions interdependent team members need to ask are:

   a. What are our specific goals, and do they align with the goals of the department?

   b. Where are we reaching are goals?

   c. What do we need to do to reach our goals?

   d. What are the specific steps for reaching our goals?

   e. How do we know when we have reached our goals?

   f. Are we all in agreement on our direction?

   g. Can we all commit to these goals?

   h. Who determines our goals and priorities?

   i. With what other organizational goals or policies must we coordinate our goals and priorities?

   j. Do we all believe we are working on the right goals?

4. *Procedure* includes decision making, problem solving, managing (including managing perceptions and cultural differences), evaluating, setting agendas, and running meetings. The questions interdependent team members need to ask are:

   a. Do we make decisions as a team or do certain individuals dominate?

   b. How well do we follow up on decisions and implement plans?

   c. Do we listen to everyone's opinions? Can we cite examples?

   d. What is our process for solving problems?

   e. How are our meeting agendas set?

   f. How do we evaluate our own individual and team performance?

   g. What are the ways we recognize each other's efforts?

   h. How are our meetings run? Are they stimulating? Useful?

i. Do we make the best use of our time or do we need to make some changes?

j. Are we too formal and rigid in how we do things? Can we cite any specific examples?

k. Are we flexible enough to change procedures in order to be more creative and innovative?

l. Do we step back occasionally to examine our meeting process? Do we need an outsider to observe our meetings and give us feedback?

There are four major cues that should be an immediate signal to managers that their team members are not working interdependently. These cues are:

1. Disagreements and conflicts are not being addressed.

2. Results are not being achieved.

3. There is much confusion about who is supposed to do what.

4. Team members are beginning to talk about each other in negative ways.

Interesting Work. If a team member finds her job interesting and feels that she is learning each day, then she will want to come to work and be motivated while she is there. Tom Peters, the management guru, once said that when you get your people to believe that they are building their résumés by coming to work each day, then you will have the most motivated people imaginable. If you, as the manager, want to have a team member motivated by the work she does, try implementing the following practices:

✔ *Give the job variety.* When a team member has to do the exact same job day after day, she will become bored and may even burn out.

✔ *Make the job as challenging as possible.* If the job is too easy the team member will lose interest and her self-worth will decrease.

✔ *Change the job on occasion.* Do some cross-training, so the team member can learn other tasks and become familiar with what happens in other areas of the company.

✔ *Make the job valuable.* Let the team member know how her job is helping the department or the organization meet its goals.

✔ *Provide learning opportunities.* Send the team member to training programs and courses or provide for online learning so she can develop more technical knowledge and expertise.

✔ *Make the job fun.* Ask the team member how the job could be more fun and follow up on as many of those suggestions as possible.

Advancement. Another motivator that builds self-worth is the opportunity for advancement. Individuals get motivated when they work hard and are appreciated for it. One of the best ways that managers can show this appreciation is to advance their team members. Advancement, in today's work world, can mean either moving to a higher level of responsibility or moving laterally. Because of decreasing levels of management, it is more difficult to promote team members than it used to be. There are just not enough slots to move people into. Therefore, managers also have to concentrate on advancing their team members through growth and learning opportunities. All managers need to have a career development plan for each of their team members in order to prepare them for either type of advancement.

The Jason McGuire Case

Picture the perfect team member. That is Jason McGuire. His performance didn't go unnoticed. After two years at Dimensional Inc., Jason had received two promotions. First, he went from a staff position to an assistant manager. He was never an accidental manager because his company spent six months training him before he was promoted, and he had the desire to manage people as well. Then, a few months ago, he moved in to the managerial role. Jason is motivated by many things, but his prime motivator is advancement. He is currently considered to be an excellent manager. But this is the end of the road for Jason. There are only two levels above him and neither of the individuals holding those slots are going anywhere, as far as anyone knows. It would be very easy for Jason to lose his motivation now. He hasn't. The president of the company has explained the realities to him and is making every effort to expose Jason to new learning and growth opportunities. He knows that he may not be able to hold on to Jason forever, but he will try to keep Jason motivated as long as Jason works for Dimensional Inc. Jason plans on using his new learning to move the company in a new direction. He hopes he will be in charge of that new division.

Motivational Dos and Don'ts for Managers

1. *Remember that what motivates people is always changing.* Today, a team member may be focused on self-worth needs. Tomorrow, she can go out and buy a new house with a big mortgage. Then the need for job security and a higher salary becomes much more important. Furthermore, what motivates one team member may not motivate another person. One team member may be motivated by public recognition, while another might be motivated by the one-to-one feedback that he gets from his manager. Managers need to individualize their motivational strategy as much as possible.

2. *Find out what motivates each team member.* There are ways that managers can find out which components of motivation a team member desires. The manager can observe the behaviors and actions of the team member; that may give some clues. Or the manager can listen to some of the statements that the team member makes. For example, if someone says to you or others on the team, "How much longer can I keep doing what I have been doing for the last three years? It is beginning to drive me crazy," then you know that team member needs some new opportunities or challenges. The most expedient method is to talk directly to your team members and ask them what they are looking for—what they need—to be more motivated.

3. *Don't let values and assumptions get in the way of providing a motivating environment.* Managers often make decisions based on their values and assumptions. When they do so, they are not seeing clearly what really motivates each of

their team members. They are seeing motivation only from their point of view.

The Case of the Nursing Assistant

At a large medical center in Houston, Texas, one of the best nursing assistants the center ever had was Angela. Patients would come back and visit her; she would get cards and presents. The story was that when patients checked in for elective surgeries, they would ask to be put in her wing. Angela had worked in this 5,000-bed facility for over five years, always getting glowing reviews from her supervisors.

Eventually, the director of nursing took notice of Angela. As a surprise and reward for Angela, the nursing director pulled a lot of strings and got Angela into nursing school without having to take any entrance examinations. The director even got her a nursing scholarship. As a result of these great deeds, what do you think Angela did? She quit her job and became a nursing assistant at another hospital. The medical center lost one of its most valuable team members.

The nursing director made two fatal mistakes. First, she applied her motivational values to another person. She thought that any nursing assistant would, of course, want to become a nurse. But that's not always true. Perhaps at this time in her life Angela was happy being the assistant, or what really motivated her was the recognition she was receiving, not the opportunity for advancement. The second mistake the nursing director made was not speaking directly to Angela or having Angela's supervisor speak directly to her.

4. *Don't punish your excellent performers.* Many managers and organizations punish their best performers each day and usually don't even know that they are doing it. When excellent performers get punished for being excellent, they will stop performing at high productivity stages. Punishing excellent performers leads to an unmotivating work environment. You are probably thinking that this makes no sense: Why would a manager and/or an organization punish their best? Here are a few examples of why it happens:

✔ *The best performers get more work to do, usually the same type of work.* When your best performers finish their regular assignments, do you say: "You're done and it's only two o'clock; that's great. Take ten more to do." It is much better if you give them new projects or new learning opportunities instead.

✔ *Top performers are held to different standards.* Managers expect their best performers to be perfect and make no mistakes. When they do make a mistake, they are often treated much more critically than others who make many mistakes.

✔ *Top performers are taken for granted.* Because they always perform well, their managers assume that they will continue to. Managers also fail to give their best performers as much positive feedback as they deserve. They may also get the most difficult shifts, be assigned to the more undesirable locations, or get the most challenging employees because the manager knows and trusts that they can handle it.

✔ *Managers don't let their top performers leave.* Managers come to overly rely on their excellent performers. I've known managers who wouldn't let their best performers go to conferences or training classes. If they are gone, who's going to do all of the work? Some managers may even try to prevent their outstanding performers from getting a promotion.

✔ *Managers don't always reward their top performers.* Team members who exceed their goals and outperform their colleagues should be rewarded. If they are not, the excellent behaviors and performance will diminish.

5. *Don't reward poorer performers.* This key point about motivation is the opposite of the previous point. When managers and organizations reward poor performance, it has a tremendous negative impact on all those staff members who are doing well. It also sends the message that the manager and/or the organization condones poor performance or behavior. Managers need to help their poorer performers improve, not reward them for not doing what they are expected to. Here are a few examples of how poorer performers get rewarded in the workplace:

✔ *They keep getting paid.* Not only do they keep getting their salaries (which are probably the same salaries as their better-performing peers earn), but they also get the annual raise and any cost-of-living increases.

✔ *They have it easy.* Because they cannot handle the job, poor performers get easier assignments, better shifts, choicer locations, and more resources.

✔ *They get promoted.* The ultimate reward for the poor performer is a promotion. Some managers don't want to deal with poor performers. They don't want to have to give them constructive feedback, document their performance, or discipline them. To make their own lives easier, some managers would do anything to get them out of their group, even if it means an undeserved promotion.

The Ronald Ackerman Case

Tamara Livingston is a manager at a well-known manufacturing company in Minnesota. Five years ago one of her employees was Ronald Ackerman. Ronald was a challenging employee. His work was competent but he had a terrible attitude. He would not share information with his teammates, failed to attend team meetings, and called people idiots to their faces. He felt he knew more than anyone else. Tamara was a new manager at the time and, overall, was handling her new responsibilities well. However, she just couldn't deal with Ronald. She had a few feedback sessions with him, but he was totally uncooperative. She decided not to get an ulcer over the whole thing and gave him a much better rating than he deserved on his performance appraisal. When Ronald viewed the job openings on the company's intranet, he saw a position that he liked, applied for it, and got it. It was at another location and a higher level. To make a long story short, for the last five years everyone at this company has been doing the same thing with Ronald. No one has wanted to deal with his unprofessional behaviors. He is now a departmental director. The irony of the story is that after the last company reorganization, Tamara now reports to Ronald, and he is making her life miserable.

She deserves it. She should have done something about his behaviors when he was her direct employee. Instead, she rewarded him for his poor behaviors.

Fifteen Ways to Make Work Fun

When team members are relaxed and having fun, the chances of creating a motivated environment are much better. Managers can bring fun to the workplace in several ways:

1. *Set aside a fun room or cubicle.* Many companies have a room where staff can go when they are feeling stressed out or need to get a few laughs. Outfit these rooms with games, comedy videos, joke books, etc.

2. *Do the unexpected.* Walk into your next staff meeting backward, or when a team member asks where the luncheon is say, "I don't know, I have eaten already." Do it in the spirit of levity.

3. *Have a fun squad.* Their mission is to find ways that the team can have fun together at work. Managers need to give everyone a chance to be on the fun squad.

4. *Don't postpone fun.* Managers may plan ways for their teams to have fun, whether it's at the office party or the off-site next month. Also, try to allow your team members some fun on the job each day.

5. *Meet informally.* Once in a while have a meeting outdoors or at a local coffee shop. Team members will be more relaxed and more communicative in the informal setting. Personal barriers between team members will also break down. Have some treats at the meeting as well.

6. *Schedule a 2:00 joke.* Gather your team together at 2:00 P.M. each day for one or two minutes. Have a different team member tell a joke each day. This little tactic will reenergize your team, especially at a time in the afternoon when people's productivity may be in a lull.

7. *Have a Friday party.* Ask your team members to work fifteen minutes longer each day and then on Friday at 4:00 P.M. have a party—or let the staff leave early.

8. *Hold competitive games.* Bring your group together and ask them to develop an original competitive game that two or more people can plan. They can use any materials or resources from their desks or from the office. They will have

fun developing these games and a blast playing them. Give out some token prizes.

9. *Hold a laugh contest.* Have your team members keep a log of how many good laughs they have each week. They have to record what made them laugh. The laughs have to be belly laughs. The team takes the winner out to dinner at the end of the month.

10. *Create a grab bag.* Each team member has to bring in a prize for under $2. The prizes have to be silly and get laughs. They have to be wrapped. Put all the prizes in a big box. Team members pick someone else's prize.

11. *Hold brainstorming sessions for fun.* Ask your team to brainstorm a new service or product that currently does not exist but will make millions of dollars. Or let them dream up new uses for an old toothbrush. Or have them "problem solve" a unique situation: What would happen if tomorrow morning everyone in the world woke up two feet shorter? What problems would the world have? Or what are the advantages and disadvantages of a five-year renewable marriage contract?

12. *Have a spelling bee.* Make a list of all the technical words that the company uses and then have a spelling bee. The winner gets a prize.

13. *Practice creativity exercises.* To stimulate thinking before an actual problem-solving meeting, engage the team in a couple of creativity-building exercises. Ask them to take thirty seconds to list everything in the room that is less than one pound. Or ask them to make a list of everything that is round.

14. *Have a fun networking bulletin board.* Encourage your team members to let others know if they are planning a fun activity and want others to join in. A team member posts her idea, the time, place, cost, etc. on the bulletin board and those who are interested respond to her directly.

15. *Establish a money jar.* Collect enough money to have a dinner or go to a sporting event. Every time someone is being negative about work—vocally or in a more subtle way—they have to put a dollar in the money jar.

Chapter Summary

Motivating is the last of the four Platinum skills. (The other three were developing others through training and delegation, active listening, and giving and receiving feedback.) Building an environment that motivates team members is the responsibility of (1) the organization, (2) the organization working with its managers, and (3) the individual manager. A motivational environment can never be created unless the organization has done its part. The organization supplies the foundation for motivation by providing a secure workplace, maintaining good working conditions, offering competitive salaries, and creating a good company image. The organization and its managers, jointly, need to provide for excellent supervision, rewards, social opportunities, and workplace practices that treat team members fairly. The manager's role is to build the self-worth of each team member. Self-worth comes from being recognized for achievements, being able to work both independently and interdependently, having interesting work to do, and having the opportunity for advancement. Finally, managers who have a positive attitude and create a fun atmosphere stand a better chance of fostering a motivated environment.

CHAPTER 8

How Organizations Can Turn Accidental Managers Into Successful Ones

This last chapter of *The Accidental Manager* looks at the impact that organizations have on creating unsuccessful managers and what they need to do to create successful ones. Then we return to the case of Andy Mercado, the story that opened the book, to see what happened to Andy when he went to work for a new organization and how he transformed into a successful manager.

Many companies and organizations are guilty of creating accidental managers. Even worse, they cause them to become unsuccessful. And even worse than that, they blame them for being unsuccessful. However, these same companies and organizations need to take a large part of the responsibility for having unsuccessful managers, accidental or not. Unsuccessful managers negatively impact their organizations' productivity and/or profitability by:

- ✔ Lowering the morale of their team members
- ✔ Increasing team member turnover
- ✔ Increasing unproductive conflicts
- ✔ Hurting the company's image
- ✔ Increasing stress levels, which results in a greater number of medical claims, grievances, and absences

✓ Minimizing concerns about quality and quantity

✓ Failing to develop the skills and talents of their team members

Hopefully, organizations may want to rethink their role in fostering unsuccessful managers by taking advantage of the following suggestions:

Suggestion 1: Give people the necessary skills before promoting them to a managerial job. The majority of organizations would never think of promoting individuals who do not have the necessary technical skills or background. Why not make sure they have the Platinum skills as well? As we know, the Platinum skills are developing others through training and delegation, active listening, giving and receiving feedback, and creating a motivational environment. These Platinum skills are often called the "soft" skills. Actually, they are the "hard" skills for someone who has not used them before or thought that they were important.

Organizations tend to wait until individuals have been in the management position for months or years before they provide any sort of training in Platinum skills. Organizations should not assume that just because someone is technically proficient, he would be a successful manager. There would be fewer unsuccessful managers if this "soft" type of training were provided before people are promoted into the managerial ranks. Then individuals would realize early on whether management is something they are suited for and want to pursue. Or they would feel more comfortable taking on the management role because they would be better equipped with the necessary skills and understanding.

Suggestion 2: Make managing a priority. If an organization wants to develop successful managers, it needs to have its new managers focus strictly on managing for the first several months. During this time managers can develop their Platinum skills. If new managers have technical tasks, projects, or assignments to do during this learning period, their management skills will take a backseat. Not having effective Platinum skills directly correlates with thinking and behaving like an unsuccessful manager.

Suggestion 3: Have a dual-track system. There are many superb staff members who do not want to be, or may not have the inclination or skill set to be, successful managers. That should be acceptable to the organization. These individuals are invaluable resources and would be of more value to the organization if they didn't become managers and have to take on new sets of skills.

Many organizations now have dual-tracking systems. These systems allows technically superior staff members to get salary increases, promotions, new titles—all the advantages of what a manager would get—without having to take on any managerial responsibilities. The dual-track system allows team members to successfully contribute to company goals, keeps them productive and happy, and increases their loyalty. If they were promoted into a managerial role, the organization would lose a valuable performer and may not get a good manager.

Organizations must not assume that everyone would welcome a managerial responsibility. Individuals have different strengths, and for many, managing is not a strength and may never be one.

Suggestion 4: Promote the managerial role. Organizations need to promote the internal benefits of managing. Team members know that managers receive more money, have more decision-making power, and get many rewards and perks. These are the external benefits. The internal benefits include:

✔ Seeing others grow, develop, and change

✔ Knowing that as managers, they can make a difference in others' lives

✔ Seeing their efforts materialize—through new processes and procedures, improved products and services, and meeting the needs of the community

✔ Enjoying the job and looking forward to coming to work each day

Internal benefits give team members additional reasons to pursue a managerial role. Organizations can promote or "sell" the internal benefits of managing by distributing articles on managing and leading, having well-known managers speak to the staff (in person or on video), publishing articles in the company's newsletter on the importance of managing effectively, or having managers at all levels within the company testify to the internal benefits they have received from managing.

Suggestion 5: Involve senior managers in the training. One of the best ways to quickly send the message that the Platinum skills are essential and that the organization expects its managers to use them is to have senior managers speak about their importance. Another way that senior managers can be role models is to have them involved in the management-training program that the company sets up. They can open the training program, have lunch with the participants, or actually conduct part of the training.

Suggestion 6: Hold managers accountable. Once managers have been trained and provided with all opportunities to succeed in the managerial role, hold them accountable if they do not do what they were trained to. If we do not hold individuals accountable they may think that what they are currently doing is acceptable. Organizations don't want to send that message.

An excellent strategy for holding managers accountable is for organizations to have a 360-degree feedback program. In this type of program, managers not only get evaluated by their bosses on their Platinum skills, but they also get evaluated by their direct employees, their peers, and their internal and/or external customers. If everyone is saying the same thing, the manager quickly gets the message.

Suggestion 7: Recognize successful managers. Let everyone in the organization know that the work of excellent managers is valued. Give managers recognition in the company paper or at general meetings, and have their pictures in lobby displays. Many organizations allow managers to be chosen the employees of the month.

Suggestion 8: Assess potential managers. Organizations that encourage individuals to succeed in their managerial roles often send their prospective managerial candidates to assessment centers. At these centers, prospective managers are given a battery of instruments and tests to determine if they have the inclination and ability to succeed as managers. Sending someone to an assessment center is a costly venture; on the other hand, not doing so can cost a company more in the long run in turnover costs and productivity losses.

The Andy Mercado Case: One Year Later

As you may recall from Chapter 1, Andy, an excellent engineer, was promoted to a managerial position when his boss left the company. Andy was promoted because he had all of the necessary technical skills, he was well liked by his other team members, and he was next in line for the promotion. Andy didn't really want the position, but he felt the organization expected him to take it and, being a new father of twins, he could use the extra money that came with the promotion. Andy became an accidental manager.

Andy found the job of managing quite difficult. He wasn't sure how to manage. He was more comfortable doing the technical work that he enjoyed. And he missed the friendship and camaraderie of his former teammates. Andy was never given any training on how to manage, nor was there any other manager available to him to give him advice.

Andy turned into a bad manager because he did not know how to be a successful one. Sometimes he would avoid his staff and not communicate with them. At other times he would knock the role of the manager, openly, in front of his staff. Then he would try to be his staff's best friend. Andy was very inconsistent in his approach. After several months as manager, Andy quit and found a staff position at another company.

Andy was very happy to be back doing only the technical work again and also liked his boss and new teammates. He missed the extra money he was making as a manager but was much more content at work and at home. About six months into this new job, Andy was approached by his manager and a representative from the human resources department. They wanted Andy to become part of a management development program. The program was designed to prepare staff members for future management positions. Andy immediately replied with a firm "no" and said he was very happy doing his current job. Nevertheless, they asked Andy if he would be willing to listen to them explain the program in more detail. Andy agreed. First, they told Andy why they felt he would make a good managerial candidate. They cited specific reasons and gave many examples from Andy's recent performance. Then they mentioned how Andy would be trained to learn management skills before he was ever promoted. They also told him that for the first few months after becoming manager, he could devote 100 percent of his time to managing and not have to worry about having his own assignments or projects to do. They explained the salary increase and the additional benefits and perks that came with the job. But they also spoke about the impact that managers could have on their team members and how team members need a manager's guidance to help them grow and develop.

This was beginning to sound very good to Andy. He did have one major objection, however. Andy said, "If I take on this managerial role, and it sounds like you are so much more serious about it than my last employer, I will miss the technical work that I so love to do." His manager and the human resources rep understood his concern and were glad that Andy brought it up. They explained that once a manager learns how to manage well and becomes successful at managing, he will have the time to work on his own projects and keep up with the latest changes in his technical field. They did emphasize, however, that managing others was still the prime responsibility that Andy would have. They asked Andy to think about it and to speak to individuals who were currently enrolled in the management development program and to managers, like his boss, who had gone through the program. They mentioned to Andy that once he began the program he would be assigned a mentor. The mentor would be there to help him learn and practice the skills he would be learning and to give guidance and support in any areas that Andy requested.

Andy thought about their proposal and spoke to several others who were in or had graduated from the program and were now managing. They all gave him a very different perspective on managing than the one he held. He now viewed successful managing as having a vital role in the success of any department or organization. He also discussed the opportunity with his wife. They both agreed that Andy should give it a try. They strongly believed that what had happened to him at his previous company wouldn't occur here.

Andy is currently enrolled in the management development program and is finding it useful and enjoyable. He is learning the necessary skills to move into management one day soon. He is also getting a new perspective on the company's business and short- and long-term goals and how the work he does fits into those goals. Andy is feeling confident that what he is learning will make him a successful manager.

Andy is learning how to complete certain forms and do all other administrative work that comes with the managerial job. Most important, he is learning skills that will help him manage his team members. He now knows the difference between leading and managing and realizes that both of these are his responsibilities. He knows that the more managing and leading he is able to do, the more successful his team members will become. He knows that if his team members become successful he will also be successful and, in turn, so will the department and the organization. Andy now knows what management and leadership skills make team members successful. They are the Platinum skills discussed in this book.

It is apparent that Andy has changed his views on managing. His days of being an accidental manager are long behind him. Andy has learned the ingredients of what it takes to be a successful manager.

Appendix A: Managerial Assessment

This appendix includes an assessment profile for you to use to ascertain how successful you are, or could be, as a manager. The assessment is based on the Platinum skills discussed in this book: developing others through delegation and training, active listening, giving and receiving feedback, and creating a motivational environment.

Read each statement in the assessment profile and indicate whether you always do, usually do, sometimes do, rarely do, or never do what each statement says. Assign a number value from the rating scale for each choice and put the number value (from 1 to 5) in the space at the end of the statement. When you have completed this assessment, add up all your numbers and determine how successful you are (or would be) in a managerial role. Then take a look at the interpretation section to see what your score means.

Rating Scale

Number Value	Meaning
5	You *always* do what the statement says.
4	You *usually* do what the statement says.
3	You *sometimes* do what the statement says.
2	You *rarely* do what the statement says.
1	You *never* do what the statement says.

The Assessment Profile

1. I make the time to develop my team members so they can become better performers. _____

2. I do not become defensive or attack my team members when they give me constructive feedback about my own actions or behaviors. _____

3. I do not have someone else discipline, coach, or do performance reviews for my team members. I do all of that myself. _____

4. If I were asked by management not to share confidential information, I would not do so with my team members. _____

5. I try new strategies and techniques to improve my working relationships with all of my team members. _____

6. I give myself positive feedback when I do well at work. _____

7. I have a very clear picture of what I want my team to accomplish at work. _____

8. I get excited and elated when my team members' results have achieved what I desired. _____

9. I carry through on the promises I make to my team members. _____

10. I know the skill and motivational levels of each of my team members. _____

11. I try to improve both the skill and motivational levels of all my team members. _____

12. I believe my main function, as a manager, is to help my people succeed. When they succeed, the organization succeeds. _____

13. When I train team members, I describe the importance of the skill that they are learning and how that skill helps the department or the organization reach its goals. _____

14. When training team members, I make sure that they can demonstrate that they have learned the new skill or behavior. _____

15. When delegating, I have the ultimate responsibility for the success of the project. I do not blame my team members if the project does not succeed. _____

16. My team members know how to proceed with their assignments and projects. _____

17. I always think about delegating. I delegate as often as possible. _____

18. When delegating, I set up periodic reviews to guarantee that the team member has grasped and is carrying out his or her new responsibilities. _____

19. Listening is a very difficult skill and I practice getting better at it. _____

20. I inspire my team members to do more than what is expected of them. _____

21. When I listen to my team members, it is important for me to be empathetic. I allow them to talk without having to feel that they are being criticized or judged. _____

22. I do not give my team members mixed messages. I would not say, "Thanks for finishing the Sondheim project on time; it saved us a lot of money by coming in ahead of schedule. But, while working on a project, you need to cut down on your numerical errors." _____

23. When I listen, I try to clarify what my team members have said. I do this to let them know that I do hear what they are saying. _____

24. I keep an open mind and try to understand the point of view of the team member. _____

25. When listening, I give my full attention to my team members. I am not on the phone, writing, or thinking about something else. _____

26. I summarize at the end of a conversation or discussion. _____

27. I am careful not to allow the words or expressions that I use to get in the way of my team members understanding me. I avoid jargon, slang, and acronyms. _____

28. I want my team members to be creative and think of new and better ways of doing their work. _____

29. When I listen, I look for meaning not only from what my team members are saying, but also from their facial expressions, hand gestures, body language, vocal tones, and inflection. _____

30. I am aware that team members come from different backgrounds and diverse cultures, so they communicate differently. I never make value judgments as to what is the best way to communicate. _____

31. I communicate my feelings and thoughts about work issues and policies to my team members. _____

32. I make it a point to give my team members positive feedback often. _____

33. I am very specific when I am describing what team members did well or what they need improvement in. I would not use a general, vague statement like, "You have a bad attitude." _____

34. I give constructive feedback in private. _____

35. I give positive or constructive feedback as soon after an event as possible. _____

36. I prefer to allow team members to come up with their own action plans for improving their work performance or work behavior. _____

37. I spend a great deal of time at work focusing on how to make my unit, group, or department better. _____

38. I am in a positive frame of mind when giving team members feedback about mistakes and errors they have made. _____

39. I try to be the best manager that I possibly can. _____

40. When I reward my team members, I do it fairly and base it strictly on performance criteria and not on what I value or who I like. _____

41. One of my goals is to develop each of my team members so he or she can work on his or her own without close supervision. _____

42. I make it a point to build a team spirit where all members work well together. _____

43. I try to provide learning and growth opportunities for each of my team members. ____

44. I build a team environment that is fun and enjoyable. ____

45. I establish ways for my team members to measure their own progress so they do not always have to rely on me to tell them how they are doing. ____

46. I am there to help team members resolve conflicts, when needed. ____

47. I match the task to be delegated to the individual's level of knowledge, skill, and interest. ____

48. I celebrate, and encourage my team members to celebrate, their successes. ____

49. I know when I am making assumptions about others, and I validate my assumptions before acting on them. ____

50. I actively communicate my support for organizational policies and procedures, even if I do not agree with them. ____

Total score ____

Interpretation

Each of the fifty items from the assessment represents a specific skill that successful managers practice on a regular basis. Review each of the items to see if you scored it a 1, 2, or 3. If you did, you need to develop an action plan for how you will improve upon this skill.

Based on your total score, this is your assessment profile:

225–250. You are in the right job and are doing (or understand) exactly what a successful manager needs to do. Your team members appreciate and value you. You are a credit to your organization.

200–224. You are well on your way to succeeding in your managerial role. You understand what it takes to be a successful manager. Keep up the good work.

175–199. You understand what it takes to succeed as a manager but need to improve the areas where you scored below a 4 on any of the items.

150–174. You need more skill development and an increased understanding of what successful managers do. Attending some training programs and reading up on successful managers would be very helpful. Additionally, speak with managers you know who enjoy their job and are good at it. They will be able to give you a lot of advice and suggestions.

Below 150. You need a great deal of management training and have to make a dedicated commitment to developing management skills. You need to acknowledge that managing is not for everyone. You may bring more value to your organization if you took a different career path.

Index

absenteeism, 53
accidental managers
  All-Time Worst Manager List,
    17–34
  "do nothing" rule and, 35–48
  myths concerning, 11–15
  options of, 10
  as successful managers,
    159–165
accountability
  of employees, 54
  of managers, 162
Ackerman, Ronald (case study),
  155
acknowledging, 88–89
  defined, 88
  examples of, 88–89
  nonverbal communication in,
    88–89
action plans, in constructive
  feedback/coaching, 111–112,
  116, 119
active listening, 83–91
  acknowledging in, 88–89
  clarifying in, 87–88
  defined, 71, 83
  habits of effective listeners,
    83–86

  maintaining congruence in,
    90–91
  self-disclosure in, 89–90
  see also Platinum skills
advancement, 151–152
agreement, in giving feedback,
  116, 119
All-Time Worst Manager List,
  17–34
  Best Friend, 23–25
  Braggart, 30–31
  Deceiver, 31–32
  Exaggerator Congratulator,
    33–34
  Limelight Taker, 25–27
  Management Knocker, 19–21,
    77
  Noncommunicator, 18–19
  Self-Castigator, 27–29
  Task Manager, 21–23
  Waffler, 29–30
American Express, 85
appreciative listening style, 82–83
articulation, 92
assessment centers, 162
assumptions, in motivation
  process, 152–153
AT&T, 102

attacking, in responding to
    feedback, 122–124
attention getting stage, 51–54
    behaviors/actions in, 51–52
    illustrations and managerial
        actions, 52–53
attitude, *see* positive attitude
authority
    cultural differences and, 96–97
    in delegation process, 67
avoiding, in responding to
    feedback, 122–124

behavior problems, in constructive
    feedback/coaching, 109
BellSouth, 102
Best Friend managers, 23–25
"big head" syndrome
    Braggart managers and, 30–31
    Limelight Taker managers and,
        25–27
blame, eliminating, 45
Blanchard, Ken, 100
body language, 93–94
    acknowledging through, 88–89
    cultural differences in, 93–94
    tips for improving, 94
bonuses, 137, 139
Braggart managers, 30–31
brain physiology, as listening
    problem, 73, 77
brainstorming sessions, 157
burnout, fallacy of omnipotence
    and, 13

cafeteria plans, for rewards,
    137–139
calmness, 131
Carter, Jimmy, 73
clarifying, 87–88
    benefits of, 87
    in constructive feedback/
        coaching, 110
    defined, 87
    examples of, 87–88
coaching, *see* constructive
    feedback/coaching

comfort level, in managing, 11
commenting, in constructive
    feedback/coaching, 109–110
commitment
    in constructive feedback/
        coaching, 110
    in delegation process, 67–68
    demonstrating, 46
committee of people, as listening
    problem, 72–73, 77
communication
    in constructive feedback/
        coaching, 109–110
    cultural differences in, 95–97
    in delegation process, 67
    of intentions, 46
    NonCommunicator managers
        and, 18–19
    nonverbal, 81, 84, 91–95
    of vision, 46
    see also listening
compensation
    fringe benefits, 134
    salary level, 135
comprehensive listening style,
    78–79
confidence, 46, 131
conflict, Best Friend managers
    and, 23–25
congruence, 94
    in active listening, 90–91
    in giving feedback, 105–106
constructive feedback/coaching,
    109–121
    action plans in, 111–112, 116,
        119
    communication skills in,
        109–110
    examples of, 110–112, 117–121
    as exception to "do nothing"
        rule, 42–43
    reasons for not giving, 112–114
    responding to, 122–124
    tips for giving, 114–116, 121
    tips for receiving, 124–125
corporate culture, "do nothing"
    rule and, 41–42

courage, 130
creativity exercises, 157
credibility
    building, 47
    feedback and, 104, 106–107,
        112–113
critical interventions, 141–142
cross-training, 150
cultural differences
    body language and, 93–94
    in listening process, 95–97
    see also corporate culture
current work, maintaining, 13–14

Davenport, Giselle (case study),
    117–121
deadlines
    active listening and, 85
    problems with, 52
Deceiver managers, 31–32
deception, Deceiver managers and,
    31–32
decision making
    independence in, 145–146
    interdependence in, 146–150
decision-making
    active listening and, 84
    self-reliance of staff and, 46–47
    Waffler managers and, 29–30
delegating, 66–68
    benefits of, 38–39
    defined, 66
    tips for effective, 66–68
determination, 131
developing team members, 39,
    49–69
    delegation in, 38–39, 66–68
    productivity stages in, 49–64
    training in, 64–66
directive listening style, 80–81
direct questions, 79–80
discipline
    as exception to "do nothing"
        rule, 42–43
    procedures for, 53–54, 114, 116
Disney Imaginary, 85
doing stage, 61–64

behaviors/actions in, 61–62
doing, defined, 36
illustrations and managerial
    actions, 62–64
dollar-limit projects, as exception
    to "do nothing" rule, 43
"do nothing" rule, 35–48
    described, 35–38
    exceptions to, 42–43
    managerial excuses for avoiding,
        40–42
    successful management and,
        44–47
    see also Platinum skills
dual-track systems, 160–161

Eisenhower, Dwight, 129–130
empathetic listening style, 81–82
enthusiasm, 130
equity of organization, 39–40
Exaggerator Congratulator
    managers, 33–34
excuses, eliminating, 45
external noise factors in listening,
    74–75
eye contact, 85, 94–95
    cultural differences in, 96
    tips for improving, 94–95

facial expression
    in listening process, 88–89,
        94–95
    tips for improving, 94–95
facial expressions, acknowledging
    through, 88–89
fact-finding listening style, 79–80
fairness
    in distribution of rewards, 139
    as motivating factor, 141–143
fallacy of omnipotence, 13
feedback
    asking for, 84
    case study on, 143
    constructive, 42–43, 109–121
    cultural differences and, 96–97
    invalid, 125–126

feedback *(continued)*
  negative, 100
  positive, 103–109, 144–145,
    154
  providing, 54, 68, 99–121
  receiving, 84, 121–126
  responding to, 122–124
  silent, 101–102
  specific, 104, 114–115, 118
  360-degree feedback program,
    162
  unclear, 126
  unrelated positive, 102–103
  valid, 125
flying blind stage, 54–56
  behaviors/actions in, 54–55
  illustrations and managerial
    actions, 55–56
fogging, 125–126
follow through, in giving feedback,
  116, 120
Friday party, 156
friends
  Best Friend managers and,
    23–25
  managing, 11–12, 13
fringe benefits, 134
fun, 131, 156–157
function, interdependence and, 148

games, 156–157
Garcia, Brenda (case study), 14
General Motors, 102
gestures
  acknowledging through, 88–89
  cultural differences in, 96
goals, in active listening, 85
grab bags, 157
growth of staff, encouraging, 39

hand gestures
  acknowledging through, 88–89
  cultural differences in, 96
hearing, listening versus, 84
human brain physiology, as
  listening problem, 73, 77
humor, 131, 156

image of company, 136
impact, in giving feedback,
  104–105, 114–115
improving, in responding to
  feedback, 122–124
independence, 145–146
individualization, of motivation
  tools, 152
integrity, 130
intentions, communicating, 46
interaction, interdependence and,
  148
interdependence, 146–150
  in function, 148
  in interaction, 148
  in procedure, 149–150
  in purpose, 149
interesting work, 150–151
internal noise factors in listening,
  74, 77
invalid feedback, 125–126

Jaffe, Michael (case study), 23–25
James, Jennifer (case study),
  21–23
job security, 134
jokes, 131, 156
Jones, Alana (case study), 30–31

laugh contests, 157
leading, defined, 36–37
Lester, Brandon (case study), 12
Limelight Taker managers, 25–27
listening, 71–97
  active, 71, 83–91
  cultural differences and, 95–97
  difficulties of, 72–77
  in giving feedback, 115,
    118–119
  habits of bad listeners, 71–72
  noise factors in, 72, 73–77
  nonverbal, 81, 91–95
  styles of, 78–83
Long, Carl (case study), 18–19
lying, Deceiver managers and,
  31–32
Lyn, Mike (case study), 29–30

Mager, Robert F., 65–66
Malcolm Baldrige awards, 50–51
Management Knocker managers,
    19–21, 77
managerial components of
    motivating environment,
    129–132, 144–155
  advancement, 151–152
  dos and don'ts for managers,
    152–155
  independence, 145–146
  interdependence, 146–150
  interesting work, 150–151
  recognition of achievements,
    144–145
managing
  assessing potential for, 162,
    167–172
  defined, 36
  as priority, 160
  promoting internal benefits of,
    161
McCord, Bob (case study), 13
McGuire, Jason (case study),
    151–152
meanings
  problem of multiple, 75–76
  of rewards, 137
  shared, 83
mentors, for managers, 47
Mercado, Andy (case study),
    7–10, 23, 163–165
micromanagement, Task Monger
    managers and, 21–23
Microsoft, 50–51, 85
money jar, 157
monitoring, in giving feedback,
    116, 120
motivation, 129–158
  feedback and, 106, 107, 115
  fun at work and, 156–157
  managerial components of,
    129–132, 144–155
  organizational components of,
    133–136
  organization/managerial
    components of, 136–143

multiple meanings, as listening
    problem, 75–76

negative feedback, 100
networking bulletin boards, 157
Nieves, Tina (case study), 19–21
90/90 rule, 102
no feedback, 101–102
noise factors in listening, 73–77
  external, 74–75
  internal, 74, 77
  multiple meanings, 75–76
  nature of, 72
  personality, 77
  values, 76–77
Noncommunicator managers,
    18–19
nonverbal communication, 81,
    84, 91–95
  acknowledging through, 88–89
  body language in, 88–89, 93–94
  congruence and, 90–91, 94
  facial expression in, 88–89,
    94–95
  proximity in, 95
  vocal listening, 92–93

Okum, Henry, 27–29
omnipotence
  "do nothing" rule and, 40–41
  fallacy of, 13
on the rise stage, 59–61
  behaviors/actions in, 59–60
  illustrations and managerial
    actions, 60–61
open-ended questions, 79
optimism, 130
organizational components of
    motivational environment,
    133–136
  company image, 136
  competitive salaries, 135
  good working conditions, 135
  secure workplace, 134

organizational/managerial
  components of motivational
  environment, 136–143
  fair treatment and, 141–143
  rewards, 137–140
  social relationships, 140–141
  supervision, 136–137
overloading, "do nothing" rule
  and, 41

pace of speech, 92
parking, 135
patience, 131
performance evaluation
  in constructive feedback/
    coaching, 109
  as exception to "do nothing"
    rule, 42–43
periodic reviews, 55, 68
perks, 137–140
personality
  feedback on, 113–114
  as listening problem, 77
personnel responsibilities, 42–43
Peters, Tom, 150
Platinum skills
  creating motivational climate,
    129–158
  defined, 16
  developing team members, 39,
    49–69
  giving and receiving feedback,
    99–127
  listening, 71–97
  overview of, 44
  promoting importance of,
    160–162
positive attitude, 129–132
  competencies in, 130–131
  reasons for importance of, 130
  techniques for maintaining,
    131–132
positive feedback, 103–109
  avoiding excuses for giving,
    106–107
  defined, 103
  examples of, 103–104

offering visibility, 144–145
  planning guide for, 108–109
  steps in giving, 108
  tips for giving, 104–109
  for top performers, 154
  unrelated, 102–103
positive self-talk, 45, 132
praise
  Exaggerator Congratulator
    managers and, 33–34
  positive feedback as, 106–107
pretending to listen, 85, 86, 93
Prince, Gary (case study), 33–34
problem solving, in constructive
  feedback/coaching, 111–112,
  116, 119
procedure, interdependence and,
  149–150
procrastination, Waffler managers
  and, 29–30
productivity stages, 49–64
  overview of, 50
  stage 1: attention getting,
    51–54
  stage 2: flying blind, 54–56
  stage 3: steadiness, 57–59
  stage 4: on the rise, 59–61
  stage 5: doing, 61–64
profit sharing, 137
promotions
  accepting in name only, 10
  accepting successfully, 10
  for poorer performers, 155
  refusing, 10
  selecting team members for,
    142, 154
  for top performers, 154
pronunciation, 92
protecting, in responding to
  feedback, 122–123
proximity, 95
public recognition, 96–97,
  107–108, 144–145, 162
public relations
  Exaggerator Congratulator
    managers and, 33–34
  offering visibility, 144–145

punishing excellence, 153–154
purpose, interdependence and, 149
Pygmalion (Shaw), 145

quarterly reviews, as exception to
    "do nothing" rule, 42–43
questions
    direct, 79–80
    open-ended, 79

rapport
    acknowledging and, 89
    and appreciative listening style,
        82–83
rate of speech, 92
relationship building, Best Friend
    managers and, 23–25
respect, Management Knocker
    managers and, 19–21, 77
reviews, periodic, 55, 68
rewards, 131, 137–140
    cafeteria plans of, 137–139
    key points for, 137–140
    for poorer performers, 154–155
    rescinding, 139–140
    for top performers, 154
Robertson, Doris, 25–27
Rosen, Bob (case study), 15

safety, 134
salaries
    level of, 135, 154–155
    for poorer performers, 154–155
    salary reviews, 42–43
Sanchez, Alan (case study), 31–32
SAS, 50–51
Schrader, Marge, 102
secure information, as exception
    to "do nothing" rule, 43
secure workplace, 134
Self-Castigator managers, 27–29
self-disclosure, 89–90
self-esteem
    feedback and, 115
    positive self-talk and, 45

Self-Castigator managers and,
    27–29
self-reliance, 46–47
self-talk, 45, 132
self-worth, 144, 151–152
Senge, Peter, 37
sensitive information, as exception
    to "do nothing" rule, 43
shared meaning, 83
Shaw, George Bernard, 145
silent feedback, 101–102
Sinclair, Kelly (case study),
    112–113
smiling, 88, 94, 132
social relationships
    Best Friend managers and,
        23–25
    as motivating factor, 140–141
Southwest Airlines, 50–51
specific feedback, 104, 114–115,
    118
spelling bees, 157
standards of performance, 65, 67,
    154
standing ovations, 131–132
steadiness stage, 57–59
    behaviors/actions in, 57
    illustrations and managerial
        actions, 57–59
stock options, 137
stress, fallacy of omnipotence and,
    13
strong will, 145
styles of listening, 78–83
    appreciative, 82–83
    comprehensive, 78–79
    directive, 80–81
    empathetic, 81–82
    fact-finding, 79–80
Sullivan, Tarj (case study), 11
summarizing, 79
supervision, as motivating factor,
    136–137
supportive skills, Task Monger
    managers and, 21–23

Task Monger managers, 21–23

team members
  developing, 39, 49–69
  friends as, 11–12, 13
  interdependence of, 146–150
  trusting, 13, 46–47
3Cs, 109–110
3M, 50–51
3Qs, Best Friend managers and,
  23–25
360-degree feedback program, 162
time
  "do nothing" rule and, 40
  feedback and, 104, 113
  setting limits in discussions, 85
timeliness, of positive feedback,
  104
time off with pay, 137, 139–140
time-outs, 132
tone of voice, 92
training, 64–66
  defined, 64
  steps in, 64–65
  tips for effective, 64–66, 162
trends, keeping up with latest, 15
trust
  acknowledging and, 89
  and appreciative listening style,
    82–83
  building, 47

feedback and, 104, 106–107,
  112–113, 115
self-disclosure and, 90
in team members, 13, 46–47

unclear feedback, 126
unrelated positive feedback,
  102–103

valid feedback, 125
values, 76–77
  cultural differences in, 95–97
  defined, 76
  as listening problem, 76–77
  in motivation process, 152–153
visibility, 96–97, 107–108,
  144–145
vision, communicating, 46
visualization, 45
vocal listening, 92–93
  components of, 92
  examples of, 93
volume of speech, 92

Waffler managers, 29–30
Walters, Barbara, 73
working conditions, 135

"you" statements, 113–114

DISCOVERY READERS®

How's the Weather?

A Look at Weather and How It Changes

240

By Melvin and Gilda Berger

Illustrated by John Emil Cymerman

HOUGHTON MIFFLIN

Boston • Atlanta • Dallas • Denver • Geneva, Illinois • Palo Alto • Princeton

The authors, artist, and publisher wish to thank the following for their invaluable advice and instruction for this book:

Jan Hyman, B.S., M. Ed (Reading), M. Ed. (Special Needs), Ed. D. (candidate)

Rose Feinberg, B.S., M. Ed. (Elementary Education), Ed. D. (Reading and Language Arts)

R.L. 2.1 Spache

ISBN: 0-618-03559-1

456789–MA–05 04 03 02 01

Library of Congress Cataloging-in-Publication Data
Berger, Melvin.
How's the weather?: a look at weather and how it changes/by Melvin and Gilda Berger: illustrated by John Emil Cymerman.
    p.   cm.—(Discovery readers)
Includes index.
Summary: Discusses how and why the weather changes and ways to predict the weather by observing the sky, clouds, and wind.
    ISBN 0-8249-8641-5 (lib. bdg.)—ISBN 0-8249-8599-0 (pbk.)
    1. Weather—Juvenile literature. 2. Meteorology—Juvenile literature.
[1. Weather. 2. Meteorology.] I. Berger, Gilda. II. Cymerman, John Emil, ill. III. Title. IV. Series.
QC981.3B47   1993
551.5—dc20   93—16686
                                                                      CIP
                                                                      AC

How's the weather?
Look at the sky.

The sun is shining.
There are few clouds.
The day is warm and sunny.

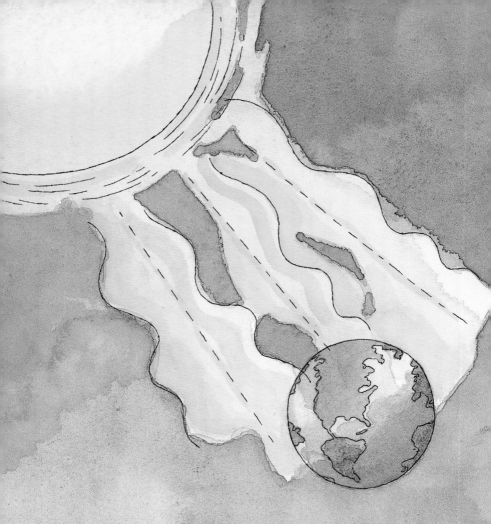

The sun is like a giant lamp in space.
It gives off rays of light and heat.
The sun's rays travel a long way to
    Earth.
Its light rays light the earth.
Its heat rays warm the earth.

We see shadows on sunny days.
Shadows form when things block the
 sun's light.
Trees, buildings, you, and I—
 we all make shadows.

During the day the sun moves across
the sky.
This makes shadows change.
They move from one side of objects to
the other.
A sundial was one of the first clocks.
It uses the moving shadow cast by the
sun to tell time.

It's fun to play outdoors on sunny days.
But the sun's rays are bad for your
skin.
Too much sun can cause a bad sunburn.
It can cause spots and wrinkles to form
on your skin when you get older.
Cover up with sunscreen!

How's the weather?
Look at the sky.

The sky is gray.
Clouds block the sun from our view.
It's a cloudy day.
What makes the clouds?

The sun's heat travels through space.
It warms the earth's oceans, rivers,
   and lakes.
Some of the water evaporates.
It becomes a gas called water vapor.
The water vapor goes up into the air.
It's there—even though you can't see it.

High up, the air is cold.
The water vapor cools.
It changes into tiny drops of water.
They form the clouds in the sky.

You can form a cloud at home.
Ask an adult to boil a pot of water.
The heat evaporates some of the water.
It changes the water into water vapor.
The hot water vapor hits the cool air.
The vapor changes into tiny drops of
    water.
They form a cloud over the pot.

Clouds in the sky have different shapes.

White, fluffy clouds are called
cumulus (KEW-mew-lus).

High, wispy clouds are called
cirrus (SERE-us).

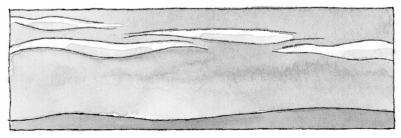

Low, gray clouds are called *stratus*
(STRAT-us).

On cloudy days, the sun is still shining.
But we cannot see the sun.
People in airplanes often fly above the
    clouds.
They can see the sun.

On cloudy days, less sunlight reaches
earth.
We do not see shadows.
Also, less heat from the sun reaches
earth.

How's the weather?
Look at the sky.

Rain is falling.
It is coming from dark gray rain clouds.
The tiny drops of water in the rain
    clouds join together.
They grow big and heavy.
They fall as raindrops.

You can make raindrops at home.
Ask an adult to boil a pot of water.
Then hand the adult a pot lid.
Ask the adult to hold the lid in the
 cloud over the pot.
Watch little drops of water form under
 the pot lid.
Soon they get very big.
Then they fall as raindrops!

Sometimes big rain clouds get a charge
 of electricity.
The electricity sends out a bolt of
 lightning.
The lightning flashes between the
 cloud and earth.
A roar of thunder fills the air.

What should you do during a lightning
 storm?
If outdoors, lie down on the ground.
Stay away from trees or lakes.
If indoors, stay away from open
 windows.
Don't use the telephone or television.

Sometimes drops of rain water freeze
   in the clouds.
They fall as snowflakes.

Go outdoors the next time it snows.
Bring along a dark piece of paper.
Catch some snowflakes on the paper.
Look closely.
All the snowflakes have six sides.
Yet no two are exactly the same!

Sometimes raindrops fall through very
cold air.
They freeze into bits of ice.
We call that sleet.

Sometimes the bits of ice get tossed
about.
Winds blow them up and down inside
the cloud.
More and more water freezes on the ice.
Finally the bigger balls of ice fall.
We call that hail.

How's the weather?
Look at the sky.

The wind is blowing.
Clouds are drifting.
Treetops are swaying.
What makes the wind?

You know that the sun warms the earth.
But some places get warmer than other
    places.
Warm air rises.
Cooler air moves in to take its place.
Moving air makes the wind.

You can make a wind too.
Take a warm shower on a cool day.
Watch the shower curtain as you turn
    on the water.
The curtain blows toward the water.
Can you guess why?

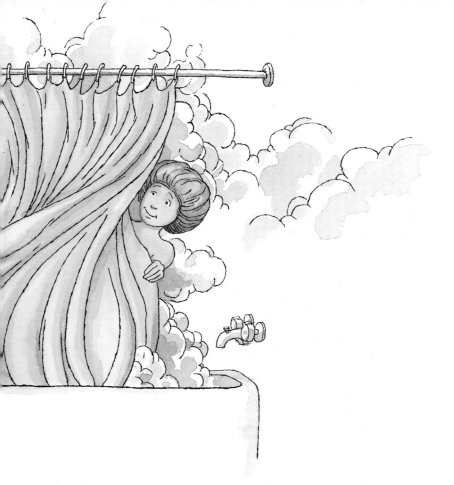

The hot water warms the air in the
  shower.
The warm air rises.
The air in the rest of the bathroom is
  cool.
The cool air rushes into the empty space.
This makes a wind.
It blows the shower curtain.

Air moves at different speeds.

When there is no wind, we say it is calm.

People call a gentle wind a breeze.

A breeze moves at about 10 miles an
hour.

We call a strong wind a gale.

Gale winds blow at about 40 miles an
hour.

Hurricanes are storms with very strong winds.

They strike mostly in warm parts of the world.

Hurricanes usually occur between May and October.

The winds start over the ocean.

They grow stronger and stronger.

The winds may reach up to 150 miles an hour.

That's as fast as a speeding race car!

Tornadoes have the strongest winds.
They mostly occur in the midwestern
  United States.
Tornadoes often start on hot, sticky
  afternoons.
Suddenly a funnel forms beneath a
  heavy, black cloud.
Violent twisting winds sweep across
  the earth.

They can spin around at 200 miles an
   hour.
That's as fast as a plane!

Hurricanes and tornadoes smash
   buildings.
They knock over large trees.
They wreck cars and big trucks.

Look at the sky.
Is it sunny, cloudy, rainy, or windy?
That's the weather today.
But what about the weather tomorrow?
The clues are all around you.
They help you know what the weather
    will be.

Is today's sunset bright and red?
Few clouds at sunset usually mean
    more fair weather.
It will most likely be sunny tomorrow.

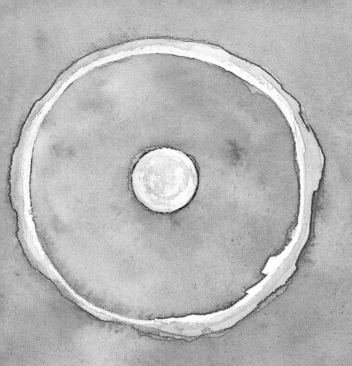

Is there a ring around the moon tonight?
Clouds may be gathering.
This usually means bad weather is
    coming.
It will most likely be stormy or rainy
    tomorrow.

Is the sky clear and the wind light
    tonight?
This usually means there will be a drop
    in the temperature.
It will most likely be cooler tomorrow.

Are there lots of clouds tonight?
A cloudy sky usually means a rise in
temperature.
The weather will most likely be
warmer tomorrow.

31

Meteorologists are scientists who study
the weather.
They measure conditions
—on the ground
—high above the earth.
They gather information from all over
the globe.
And they put the facts and figures into
huge computers.

Meteorologists then forecast the
weather.
And they prepare weather maps.
You can hear their forecasts on the
radio or television.
You can find their weather maps in the
newspaper or on television.

Many weather forecasts are correct.
But sometimes they are wrong.
Winds and clouds keep moving.
Weather conditions keep changing.
This can make the forecast wrong.

You can use a weather map to forecast
   the weather.
Weather maps show big blocks of air.
These blocks of air move over the earth.
This map shows where the air is moving.

Weather often stays the same for
   several days.
The blocks of air move slowly or not
   at all.
Then they move away.
As they move, the weather changes.

Look at this weather map.

A block of cold air is pushing against a block of warm air.

The place where they meet is called a cold front.

On the map, it is a blue line with points sticking out.

The points show the direction the cold air is moving.

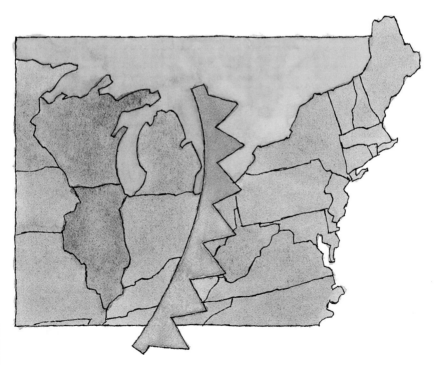

Cold fronts move quickly.
They push the warm air up and out of
   the way.
Suddenly strong winds blow.
The weather turns stormy.
Rain or snow may fall.
Thunder and lightning may come too.

Soon the cold front passes.
The sky clears.
The weather gets colder and drier.

Here is another weather map.

A block of warm air is pushing against a block of cold air.

The place where they meet is called a warm front.

On the map, it is a red line with little bumps.

The bumps show the direction the warm air is moving.

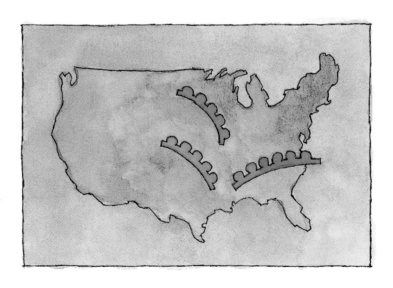

Warm fronts move slowly.
They slide over the cold air.
The winds blow gently along a warm
    front.
Light rain may fall for a few days.

Gradually the warm front passes.
The sky clears.
The weather gets sunny and warmer.

Here is another weather map.
Find the state where you live.
Is a cold front moving toward your
    state?

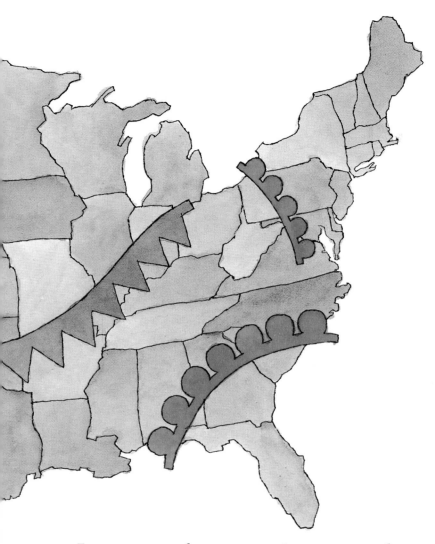

Is a warm front moving toward
 your state?
From this map, what do you think
 your weather will be?

Weather maps sometimes show air
   pressure.
Air pressure is the weight of the air on
   the earth.
You cannot feel the air pressing down.
But it is always there.
And it is always changing.

Sometimes the air pressure is low.
Air rises into the sky.
The air has water vapor.
Clouds form.
The clouds get bigger and darker.
Soon it will rain or snow.

Sometimes the pressure is high.
More air sinks to the ground.
The sky is mostly clear.
Puffy cumulus clouds may appear.
But it will not rain.
The weather will stay dry and sunny.

How's the weather?
Look at the sky.

What will the weather be?
Look at the sky—and look at a
    weather map!

Index

air, 21, 23-24, 35-39, 42-44

air pressure, 42-44

breeze, 24

cirrus, 11

clouds, 8-13

cold front, 36-37

cumulus, 11, 44

forecasts, 28-45

gale, 24

hail, 19

hurricanes, 25, 27

lightning, 16-17

meteorologists, 32-33

rain, 14-15

rays, 4, 7

shadows, 5

sleet, 19

snowflakes, 18

stratus, 11

sundial, 6

sunlight, 3-7

tornadoes, 26-27

warm front, 38-39

water vapor, 9-10, 42

weather maps, 33, 35-42

wind, 20-27